CHAPTER 1

Helen was hauling the last batch of newspapers onto the hand truck Jake had thoughtfully purchased for her last Christmas. The day was promising to be a real scorcher. Even at this early hour, the summer heat was rising from the gum-imbedded sidewalk.

"Can I help you, Mrs. Ryan?"

"No, I got it, but the friggin' news driver is gonna get it from me. He dumped all the Sunday inserts down by Doc's drugstore. He must be a real bozo."

Once inside the store, I was assailed by a plethora of odors that had intrigued me since childhood: the waxy smell of the baseball bubble gum packets, the penny candy section, the aroma of just-percolated coffee and the wooden smell of the balsa wood glider planes hanging on a string. From the back came the sounds of their daughter Pat getting her children ready for another day.

"Put on the air conditioner for me while I get you your coffee." She said to me. I go there quite frequently for my morning dose of coffee and neighborhood gossip. I've lived in Bay Ridge, all my life. I travel for business, I'm a financial advisor and if I do say so myself, I'm pretty good at it. Truthfully, I'd rather be in the candy store then in all the fancy places I take my clients to. Helen and Jake are real. If you know what I mean. Enough about me. So let me tell you the story of the Ryan's and their lives.

The revving of a turboprop jet could not compare to the sound of Ryan's air conditioner when it first started. But in a few minutes, the motor idled into the already-constant din of the ice cream freezer, the soda chest, and Jake's little icebox for his private stock.

"That damn Tommy Cool."

"Who?" I asked.

5

"Tommy Cool—you know, the little guy that fixes all the machines. The only time I see him is when he's broke and wants some coffee or cigarettes or something. He's always promising to fix that god-awful air conditioner. It would wake the dead."

"Morning, Dotty. How's Tom doing?"

"Hi, Tony. I like that tie. How's school?"

The early morning workers and churchgoers were beginning to filter in for their papers. Each was greeted personally and cordially by Helen, the uncrowned queen of Third Avenue.

In her middle fifties, she had retained most of her youthful baby fat. Her round Irish face and twinkling blue eyes never betrayed the years of struggle that lay behind her. In her younger years, she had been a beauty. Now she had a matronly shape, but it was quite evident that she had been a very pretty young woman, blessed with freckles, deep-blue eyes, and a lovely figure. Even then she had to watch her intake of calories, but it was a battle she won more than lost in her younger years.

CHAPTER 2

H elen and Jake Ryan had married thirty-five years ago. Jake, a tall thin man, was a longshoreman on New York City's waterfront, while Helen, known as Middie, waited tables in the waterfront eateries, which were frequented by her brothers and their work gang, as well as Jake and his gang.

"Many's the patch I pasted on those bums."

They'd come in at eight thirty and have a few balls and beer; some came in at nine thirty, ten thirty, and eleven thirty. By the time lunchtime came, they would really be loaded. They'd go back to the ships and fall down an open hatch and split wide open. Jake or one of her brothers would drag him up to Middie to piece back together.

"For Christ's sake, Jake, didn't you ever hear of a doctor or hospital?"

"Aw, Middie, the boss would dock him and not hire him tomorrow. He's got a wife and six kids."

"Every one of those beauts has a wife and six kids—not three or four, but always six."

Jake would volunteer to bring the injured dock walloper to Middie's first-aid station every chance he could. This little ploy enabled him to engage in his favorite sport. While Middie would be doing everything short of surgery, Jake was keeping his elbow bent, telling her what a marvelous job she was doing.

And so they were married.

CHAPTER 3

World War II was starting to cloud the European horizon. But the world for the Ryans had brightened considerably. Two daughters had been born. Jake had gotten a raise and promotion (only God knew how), and Middie was expecting again.

Jake was later than usual getting home. Helen busied herself with the girls and crooned while fixing the table for the main meal of the day. She wanted to make it special as this was their wedding anniversary. The only interruption in her routine was when she had to separate the kids with "Cut that out, girls, you little brats" or "I'll crack your ass!" But even the fighting of the kids couldn't stop her from being in a good mood. After all, she was having another child. Jake had calmed down, somewhat, and was a good provider. Yes, life looked good in Brooklyn.

The rain was rushing earthward with a fury that seemed uncontrollable. As it hit the darkened sidewalks, it formed pools of black water. The streets were rushing torrents of curbside garbage swiftly falling into the quickly filling sewers. Helen thought out loud, "My goddamn sheets are still on the friggin line!" As she hurried into the dry entrance to their six-room railroad flat, she could hear her mother yelling at the girls. So she knew everything was alright. As she placed her rain soaked bundles onto the kitchen table, she felt the first pain, but shrugged it off as a little kick from the unborn inside her.

"Where the hell is Jake? That bum is never here in time!"

"Now, Middie, don't get yourself excited. You know the waterfront's busy. Just think of all the overtime he's getting."

"He'll probably piss it away on the numbers or on a horse. Better yet, maybe one of those bums with the six kids will hit him for a touch."

"I guess you're right. The weather must be getting to me."

Then it came, another pain and another right after it. "What the hell is going on? This kid is kicking my insides out."

"I've told you not to carry all those bags up the stairs. You should leave them in the hall for Jake or one of your brothers to carry up."

"My brothers, dearest Mother, will probably be drunk and pee in the hall over my groceries."

"Now, Middie…"

The pain became excruciating. She wasn't one to cry, but this was unbearable. The doctor had told her the baby was due in May, and this was only mid-April.

"What the hell is going on?"

"What's the matter, Middie?"

"I feel like crap."

"You look lousy."

"Thanks, Mom."

"I'll take the kids downstairs, and I'll be back."

"Mom, don't go. Send someone for a cab or call the friggin in cops. This guy won't wait."

CHAPTER 4

Jake was in the rear booth of McCarthy's, counting the money he and the other gang bosses had collected for the widow of Tim Malley.

"Poor Tim Malley got himself run over by a trolley up on New Utrecht Avenue in Dago Land. Nah, he wasn't drunk. One of those wops pushed him, I'll bet."

"Jake, phone call for you."

"Who is it? If it's Middie, tell her I haven't been here, and I haven't been drinking either."

"It's her sister Jeanie."

He grabbed the phone. Jeanie said, "Jake, get over to the Norwegian right away. Something's wrong with Middie. The cops just rushed her there. I ran down to call you... Jake, are you sober?"

"Jeanie, mind your own business, and take care of the girls."

Before he could get a cab, he was soaked right to the skin. The rain was an omen to Jake. All dock wallopers hated rain. Rain meant no work on the waterfront. The steel decks became as slick as glass, and the ladders leading to the different holds were treacherous enough when dry and twice as bad when wet. Jake ran the twenty blocks to the hospital. He was dripping wet as he entered the lobby and saw his mother-in-law fingering her rosary beads.

"Mom, what happened?"

"It's terrible! It happened all of a sudden. I don't know. I just don't know."

"Mom, for Christ's sake, what happened?"

"Oh, Jake, pray for her."

"Cut that shit out. Is she dead?"

He could get absolutely nothing from his mother-in-law. The usually calm lady had gone completely into shock. Jake went to the receptionist and explained who he was and asked for information.

"I'm sorry. I can't give any information about a patient's condition."

"Goddammit, she's my wife! Now what the hell is going on?"

After what seemed an eternity, a young nurse came out of the Do Not Enter door and asked for Mr. Ryan. As Jake virtually lunged at her, he realized what he must look like. Soaking wet, dirty clothes, eyes wild with anguish, and out of breath from running.

"Are you Mr. Ryan?" she asked, raising a disapproving eyebrow. Jake nodded. He couldn't speak. "The doctor wants to see you in room 776 down the corridor to the left."

He nearly flew down the pale-green and faded white corridor. By this time, he was convinced Middie was dead. As he reached the door numbered 776, he made an effort to regain his normal composure. He knocked then entered.

"Sit down, Mr. Ryan. I'm Dr. Weiss."

A friggin Jew, Jake thought briefly. "How's my wife? What happened? Where is she? What about the baby? Level with me, Doc, is she dead?"

"Well, she isn't," the doctor said, calmly looking Jake in the eye.

Jake fought back an urge to cry, but he told himself that longshoremen didn't cry, that he was tough. When the inward conversation with himself was finished, he took a deep breath and continued, "What happened, Doc?"

"Mr. Ryan, your wife is very ill, but I feel certain that we can save her. The pregnancy has to be terminated, or there's a good possibility that your wife will die. I'll need your permission to remove the fetus. Once that's done, your wife will be out of danger, and we can be reasonably sure she'll be up and around in a few weeks. She's in great pain and not very coherent."

Jake tried to let the words sink in and figure out what they actually meant. *I left for work this morning, and she was fine, laughing, cursing, and getting the breakfast ready for the girls. Now she's in a hospital with some Jew telling me she might die. What the hell is going on?*

The doctor interrupted Jake's thoughts. "I know you're Catholic, Mr. Ryan..." *What's that got to do with anything?* Jake thought almost out loud. "But unless I get your permission to crush the fetus's skull, the fetus will—or shall I say might?—cause your wife's death."

"Crush whose skull?"

"The fetus's, the unborn baby's, Mr. Ryan."

Jake wasn't a very religious man, but he recalled the way Helen talked about this. That fetus was a baby and already had a name: Little Jake. *Oh my god, what am I doing here? I can't do this to her! Give me ten men in a gang, and I can unload a fleet of ships. Don't make me have to kill Helen's baby. I don't give a damn about religion. I'll probably go to hell anyway. Helen would never forgive me. She'd never forgive me!*

Finally, Jake said out loud, "Doc, what else can be done? I mean, like, I've heard of women that have had operations to have the baby. What's it called?"

"Cesarean section, Mr. Ryan, but it's very expensive, and it's, well, the clinic patients don't... What I mean, Mr. Ryan, is that, well, you know..."

"No, I don't know. You mean a laborer's wife doesn't mean damn, but some Mrs. Rich Bitch can have her kid and still be up and around in a few weeks. Well, listen to me, you little son of a bitch. She's gonna have that kid, and you're going to give her that Cesar... Ceasar...whatever the hell it is. You'll get your money tonight if you want! But neither you or anyone else is going to crush my kid's skull. You son of a bitch, now get in there and tell all those high-class nurses to get my Middie ready for that fancy operation, and they both better be able to have visitors tomorrow morning."

"Mr. Ryan, I didn't mean to—"

"You didn't mean shit! How much is this going to cost?"

"Well, about $900 all total."

"You get going, and I'll be back in time to hear you smack the new clinic patient on the ass. Now let's go."

"Yes, sir, Mr. Ryan. Yes, sir."

The doctor headed toward the door marked Labor Room, giving orders to nurses while cautiously looking over his shoulder at Jake, whose six-three frame seemed to fill the hallway.

CHAPTER 5

*W*here do I go from here? Where in the name of Jesus am I gonna get $900? I haven't even got $9!

Then the collection money crossed his mind. It was over $1,000. Who would know? This was an emergency. Tim would do the same if their positions were reversed. He was a no-good bastard anyway.

Hey, that's it—Tim's money!

By this time, Jake had walked back through the driving rain to the waterfront bar, McCarthy's. Once inside, he felt the chill and had four fast balls. Dan McCarthy was behind the bar.

"What's the matter, Jake? You look like someone without any friends."

Jake stared at himself in the mirror, and McCarthy's words had a special impact on him. If he took the money of Malley's widow, he'd be without friends. He'd never done anything dishonest in his life. Tim was a good man and a good friend. He did leave a wife and six little children. How could he have even thought about the collection money?

My god! he thought. He was cold.

"Give me another ball, Dan, and put it on my tab." He downed the whiskey and felt the warmth flowing through his body.

"Dan, have you seen Louie Grasso around? I got to talk to him."

"Jake, something's wrong. What do you want to see Loui about? You're not gonna borrow any money from him, are you?"

"Dan, you're a nice man, but mind your own friggin business."

"Look, Jake, if that bastard gets his hooks into you, you'll not have a paycheck of your own. How many guys have you given extra work to just to keep them away from that fat Guinea?"

McCarthy poured another one as he continued to talk. "Things can't be that bad, Jake. Let me see if I can help."

Jake downed the amber fluid in one gulp and started to recount the hospital scene to the bartender.

Dan McCarthy was bigger than Jake and about forty years older. His snow-white hair added to his deep-blue eyes, and his ever-present bow tie and white apron made him the classic picture of the Irish bartender. Dan had been widowed for more than fifteen years. Dan Jr. was a sergeant for the police department and very rarely came to Brooklyn. "After all, he has his wife and children and the house out in Rosedale. But he calls. and I know he thinks about me." That was the old bartender's rationalization of the treatment accorded him by his son and daughter-in-law.

Jake was starting to shiver as he went back to the hospital. Dan had given him the money with no strings attached. Jake hated to take it from the old man, but he had to unburden himself to someone, and Dan was a good friend. He had no idea Dan had that kind of cash around. He'd just told his problem out of a sense of frustration and from the whiskey coursing through his bloodstream. He was starting to feel better.

Once inside the waiting room, Jake grew impatient. What was taking so long? If that little Jew screwed up… No, everything would be all right. Middie was tough. What would he do without her?

"Mr. Ryan, Mr. Ryan."

"Where am I? Holy shit, I must have fallen asleep. What is it, Nurse? Is everything all right?"

"The doctor wants to see you in room—"

"Yeah, I know, 776."

Jake gathered his wits as he entered the room. Dr. Weiss was smiling as he entered.

"Congratulations, Mr. Ryan, they're all fine. I think you and I sort of got off on the wrong foot. I didn't mean to imply—"

"What do you mean *they*?"

"Your wife gave birth to twins. Didn't the nurse tell you?"

"Twins! Holy shit! Twins!"

"Yes, twins. Twin girls."

"Holy shit, Doc, twins!"

The thought crossed his mind that this little damn would want $1,800, but Jake dismissed it.

"When can I see my wife?"

"Not until 10:00 a.m., but you can see the babies now if you wish."

As he was looking at the tiny pink bundles, the thought that came into his mind nearly made him wild. *That bastard! That dirty bastard didn't know there were two—what did he call it?—fetus. Two in Middie's belly! That son of a bitch! Five hours ago, they were fetus. Now that little son of a bitch Jew calls them babies.*

Jake left the nursery area and returned in a near rage to room 776. Fortunately, Dr. Weiss was nowhere to be found, because Jake wanted to crush his skull with his powerful hands.

The rain had subsided when he woke Kathleen and Betsy to tell them the news. Both children were asleep, and their lack of enthusiasm made it quite evident that they wanted to get back to their dreams. "Aw, the little brats, what do they know?" he murmured allowed.

Kathleen was four and Betsy three. Jake had another ball and sank into the Morris chair by the radio and fell into a deep sleep. His mother-in-law, completely composed now, woke him from his sound sleep. Today was Sunday, so the waterfront was shut down, but he did have to get to the hospital. He felt lousy, but he showered, shaved, and put on his good blue suit. Then off he went.

"Goddamn you, you son of a bitch! Where have you been? Let me smell your breath."

Middie was tough, all right. Less than twenty-six hours had passed since they had seen each other, and so much had happened to them. But Helen was Helen, and twins or not, that was the greeting he received as he stooped over to kiss her.

"You did a good job, Mid."

"No thanks to you, ya big bastard."

And they both laughed and held hands until the nurse shushed them into subdued giggles.

CHAPTER 6

"Morning, Jake."

"Hi…are the papers in, Mid?"

"You know they are, you big bastard. Come and get your coffee."

"Hey, Jake, let me ask you a question," I said. "Every morning I'm here, you come out and say the same thing, and she gives you the same answer. What would you do if she didn't have the papers inside?"

"She has her job, and I have mine. I invested in that hand truck because she was starting to slow down a bit, but if they're not in, I'd probably go back to bed until she had them or wait until some silly bastard, like you, helped her with them."

"Oh," I responded. The door opened and a young man, about thirty, walked over to Jake.

"Morning, sir. I'm here as an advance man for Wonder Publications. We are trying to interest the star owners in the area to…" The sales pitch continued, then later ended with, "And so you see, sir, it is a very good offer, and I think you could make some money and so could my company."

After listening to the salesman's speech, Jake pointed down to the end of the Candy Store and said, "I only work here. I can't make any decisions, but that lady down the end, she's the boss. I know she's interested."

"I see…" The salesman went to Middie. "Morning, ma'am. I'm here as an advance man for Wonder. Publications. We are trying to interest store owners in the area to—"

"Wait a minute, did you say Wonder Publications?"

"Yes."

"So I take your comics and magazines, but I have to take some of those dirty books with the girls with their big boobs hanging out, right?"

The little salesman was starting to squirm slightly.

"Look around, mister. Look at these kids coming in here. They get into enough trouble without me having naked ladies staring them in the eye."

"But, madam, look at them. They are either Negro or Puerto Rican. Statistics prove they are of low moral character."

Helen became instantly angry. To her, they were kids—not Negro or Puerto Rican kids, just kids. When it came to children, she was color-blind.

"You sweaty little SOB! [There were children near.] I happen to be married to a colored man, and his moral character is better than yours, you smut-pedaling little bastard! [The children had left.]"

"Good day, ma'am."

After the salesman left, Helen turned to Jake and began the expected tirade.

"You friggin bastard, you send all those bums to me. What the hell is the matter with you?"

"But, Helen, you're the boss here. I'm not even on the payroll. I'm a kept man." He looked at me and winked.

It was hard for him to keep a straight face, but years of this type of teasing had made Jake a master at deadpan faces. Suddenly, Jake said, "What do you mean you're married to a colored man?" Jake seemed offended.

Helen started laughing at the hangdog look on his face. Soon everyone was laughing, including Big Jake.

CHAPTER 7

"Mrs. Hoffman! How are you this fine day?"

"Oh, Mr. Ryan, I feel wonderful. I can't believe that one year could make such a difference in a person. To think that last year I could hardly get around. Now I can do my own shopping. You see the new cart?"

"Yes, I like it. I see you have new sneakers. They're very becoming, do wonders for you."

"Oh, Mr. Ryan, you must say that to all the ladies."

"Not really. I don't know many who wear sneakers."

As she went out, Mrs. Hoffman gave one more flirtatious wink at Jake and trundled off, dragging her shopping cart behind her.

Jake continued "She is a pisser. Last year I would have bet anything that she'd be dead by now. All of a sudden, she meets this old guy, and she's a different person. At first he used to carry her packages home for her. Then he'd come around, and they'd stand in the hallway and talk. All of a sudden, they started swapping spit right by the front door. Now the bastard has moved in with her. She's a new person. They must go at it at least three times a day, and he's going to be close to seventy, and she's right near that too. She's a pisser, all right. She'll probably bury this guy, just like she did Old Man Hoffman. Here comes another beaut."

"Who's that, Jake?"

"Take a look at her," he said out of the corner of his mouth.

"Oh, hello, Gloria. Is it still club soda?"

Here was a woman about sixty years old with bleached blond hair, ruby-red lipstick, and a chest on her the size of two large melons. At first glance at her, you'd immediately think of a retired madam.

"No, Mr. Ryan, this week it's ginger ale, and you'd better give me two large bottles. Tonight's a special night."

As she left the store, Jake told me a little about Gloria the Hooker. Jake's kitchen window looks right into Gloria' s living room, separated by an alleyway that was about six feet wide. Early one morning, Jake awoke and was unable to get back to sleep. Quietly he slipped into the kitchen and, without turning on the lights, found the icebox and removed a can of cold beer. He glanced out at the sky and swore softly. He knew it was going to be a hot day, for the sky was black, dotted with twinkling blue-white stars. With the ability to predict the weather, gained from his experiences in France during the war, he developed a farmer's mind.

Pretty good for a city boy, he mused. *That Tommy Cool.*

He had promised to fix the air conditioner three days ago, but still there was no sign of him.

Oh well, there's always beer to cool you off.

He seated himself at the table next to the window and became conscious of low voices. To his surprise, Gloria hadn't pulled her shades down, and there she was, naked as a jaybird, lying on the couch against the far wall with a night light on.

Not bad for an old broad, he thought. *She's still got a mile or two left in her, I'll bet.* Feeling slightly like a Peeping Tom, he decided to check things out front of the Candy Store. *Well, one more peak won't hurt.*

As he glanced at the shadeless window, he saw a gray-haired old guy come from the vicinity of Gloria's bathroom, fully clothed.

This guy's got to be at least eighty—well, maybe seventy-five, Jake thought. The old gent bent down, kissed her, placed a bill on a table next to the couch, and left. Jake opened another beer and settled down to watch. About fifteen minutes later, he could hear a knock at the apartment door. As she opened it, Jake saw and recognized Cheapo Tim, the guy who owned the automatic laundry.

Tim was a widower and was "cheap as dog shit," as Helen put it. He'd get all the kids in the neighborhood to do odd jobs around the laundry and then wouldn't pay them the amount he'd promised. Helen despised him for that. You just didn't cheat kids.

Gloria handed Tim a drink and started to unloosen his tie.

"I don't believe this," Jake said out loud. He rushed to Helen and woke her up. After hurriedly explaining what was going on, Helen put a robe on and came out too.

"Not to be nosy, just wanted to see if Jake was seeing things. That's terrible! That's terrible!" But she kept on watching. Tim finally and, with his clothes over his arm, made his way toward the bathroom.

"See! What'd I tell you? Now I'll bet you he'll pay her."

"Oh bullshit, Jake, she's no hooker."

Tim reappeared and bent down, kissed her, and just as his predecessor before him, placed a bill on the dresser.

Gloria removed the bill and, loud enough for the unseen spectators to hear, called to Tim, "Hey, you cheap bastard, this is only a ten spot. What the hell are you trying to pull?"

"Quiet, you'll wake the neighbors."

"Screw the neighbors! You know I charge twenty, you cheap son of a bitch."

By this time, Jake was in a fit of uncontrollable laughter, Helen was trying to listen, and Tim was trying to escape the scathing tongue of Gloria the Hooker while searching for another ten-dollar bill.

The next morning, when Gloria came into the store, Jake found himself looking at her in a different light. He viewed her with a type of respect he hadn't had before. After all, how many people had a real live prostitute living next door who could get twenty dollars out of Cheapo Tim? Now that was a woman to be admired.

CHAPTER 8

The waterfront was busy, very busy. There was plenty of work and more than enough overtime to go around. But the dock boss where Jake had his gang kept placing men from Jersey instead of Jake's. This wasn't an uncommon practice, but with all the ships coming in and going, Jersey had to be as busy as Brooklyn.

Early one Thursday, Jake, as usual, stopped at the Guinea Wine Joint next to the hiring hall to have a fast shot of Scotch to ward off the morning chill. Rocco would make sandwiches and huge urns of coffee. He'd take them to the piers and sell them to the workers. Although he was only licensed to sell wine and beer in his establishment, he always had a bottle of Scotch handy for his "bigga Irisha friend, Mista Jake." Even though Rocco had been in the United States for more than thirty years, he hadn't lost his very southern Italian accent. He strongly resembled an organ grinder, sans monkey.

"Mista Jake, I'm a gotta talka to you. Itsa important."

"What's the matter?"

"Nonja go toa the halla righta now. You stay widda me."

"Rocco, what's the matter?"

"I'ma try to tella you. There's bada men ina the halla. They gonna beata Mista Dooley." Dooley was the dock boss of six piers. He was the one who was pushing all the supervisors to take the Jersey men.

"Who are those guys? And why are they after Dooley?"

Rocco started speaking, and Jake glanced out the grimy front window and saw a large black limousine parked in front of the hall. The engine was running, and he recognized Louis Grasso, the waterfront loan shark, sitting behind the wheel, puffing on his ever-present De Nobili. Jake didn't know which smelled worse, Louie's cigar or Louie himself.

Without waiting for Rocco to explain any further, he slipped out the side door, crossed the separating alley, and noiselessly entered the hall's rear door. The building itself had been constructed specifically for use as a government warehouse for the storage of coffee during World War I. The pungent bean smell still permeated the air in the early morning. Once the doors opened, the hall became filled with cigar-chomping longshoremen, blowing their bluish billows into the rafters of the old building, completely masking the coffee smell.

The interior was black, save for a lone naked bulb in the time-keeper's partitioned office. He could hear voices coming from the office area, but couldn't see anyone.

Walking silently, hardly breathing, the tall dockworker approached the lighted area. Peering through the nicotine-stained door window, Jake could see his friend Dooley with his arms pinioned by a large man that he'd never seen before. Standing in front of Dooley was Tony "One Ear" Mastrion.

Tony was a small-time hoodlum replete with his blue pinstriped suit, large flowered tie, and shiny black-and-white brogans. He was every much the well-dressed gangster. No one knew for sure, but rumor had it that he lost his ear in a confrontation with a little shoe salesman he smacked for no reason other than to bolster his ego. The diminutive clerk reached into his faded gray smock and removed a silver-handed tool with a razor blade fastened to the end. All this was many years ago. Tony's version was much more romantic. It involved a robbery, a police chase, and a lucky shot fired by some "dumb rookie cop." Jake believed the one about the shoe clerk.

CHAPTER 9

Helen was helping Erin and Tara with their morning bowl of oatmeal. The other two girls had finished and were getting into their heavy school coats for their daily trip to first and second grade. Helen marveled at what beautiful children the four of them were. Kathleen, the oldest, was barely an inch taller than Betsy. She dressed them alike and fixed their flaxen hair in long braids, festooned with gaily colored ribbons. Passersby thought she had two sets of twins. The oldest liked to confuse people by assuming each other's names. Secretly this was a source of great amusement to Helen, but she half-heartedly chastised the girls when they played their little game.

"Come on, my little ladies, you have to go. It's twenty-five to nine. Hurry up."

The girls kissed her, and she gave them a swat on the rear, which she reasoned was only a love pat.

Jake knew that if he was going to do something, the time was now. The gangs would be coming to the hall in another twenty-five minutes. He could see that Dooley had been worked over. Blood was running from his nose and mouth. His face was puffy, and crimson fluid was trickling from his ears. Tony was swearing at Dooley as he reached into his jacket and removed a pair of brass knuckles.

Dooley kept repeating, "No, no, I can't. I won't..."

Jake groped around in the darkened hall, looking for some type of club. One Ear wouldn't be a problem for him, but if the other hood had a gun, it could be ticklish. In a pile were large water-soaked beams that were used as braces, keeping the ships and barges from striking the piers. He selected one, about four feet long; took a deep breath, and kicked open the office door.

The next few minutes became a large blur. As Mastrion spun around, Jake came down with the brine-soaked beam right in the center of his head. Blood and pieces of brain immediately shot around the room, covering Jake and Dooley with gore that had an unreal quality about it. The large man was taken completely by surprise, still holding on to Dooley, who, at this point, was about to collapse.

Jake stepped over the convulsing form of One Ear and swung the bloodstained club. The large man had produced a pistol from his pocket, and the beam hit the hand with a crushing, sickening thud. The gunman started screaming. Jake dropped the club and placed his large hands around the screaming man's throat. He kept squeezing until the man fell limp, not breathing.

The room was hot and smelly. The gunman, in his last moments of life, had been unable to control his bowels.

Dooley had vomited from the beating and the horrible scene in general. Mastrion was dead where he had fallen.

Jake was startled by a noise in the doorway. He knew before he looked up from Dooley who :it was. He had forgotten about Grasso. There he was, standing there with a large blue-black automatic in his hand. Jake wasn't one for prayers, but he knew he should say some now. Suddenly, he realized that he had just killed two men and had only a vague idea as to why. What did they want from Dooley? He never got into the loan sharks. Dooley was widowed, and his only son was a priest, up for monsignor, no less. Why were they beating him up, and was this connected with the sudden influx of Jersey men?

Grasso wore a twisted smile on his face, with the ever-present stinking De Nobili stuck between his uncared for front teeth. Jake stood to his full height and was ready for the inevitable. Grasso was surveying the damage with the cool eye of a professional, checking for mistakes.

"Hey, Jake, you did a nice job, but you're typical Irish. You're a slob. Tony was a friend of mine, Jake. I don't like to see Irish kill my friends, Jake. You know that."

The rhetorical question went unanswered as Jake was busy trying to remember his childhood prayers. The best he could come up with was grace before meals. *It's a prayer—better than nothing*, he thought. Grasso was still talking to Jake. He was playing cat and mouse with him. "Goddammit, Louie, get it over with," Jake felt like saying. But he wouldn't give the greaseball the satisfaction. He stood perfectly still. Abruptly, in the middle of Jake's thoughts, Louie Grasso pitched forward, falling into the office. From his back, which was rapidly turning crimson, Jake could see the handle of a stiletto.

"Rocco! What the—"

"No tima now, Mista Jake. You go widda Mista Dooley to my place. I lefta the backa door open fora you. I fixa da place. You go now, I taka care."

CHAPTER 10

J ake knew there were others in the hall with Rocco, even though he couldn't see them. He hoisted the semiconscious Dooley onto his broad shoulders and went to the rear of the hall. As he hit the fresh air, a wave of nausea came over him. Unseen hands had placed a tarpaulin over Dooley and made Jake's cargo inconspicuous to any eyes. But the precaution was unnecessary. The alley separating the hall and Rocco's was blocked from view by a large canvass-covered truck backing in from the street.

Once inside the rear of the Italian's store, he tried to revive Dooley. The bleeding from the mouth and nose had stopped, but there was still a small trickle of crimson oozing from the old man's ears. Jake was startled as Rocco placed a firm but gentle hand over his shoulder.

"This way, Mista Jake."

He walked woodenly to the rear of the building, where a wood-shed had been converted into a storage area.

"Taka you shirt off."

Jake responded wordlessly.

"Putta this on. Drinka this."

He put on a faded blue work shirt, almost identical to the blood-soaked one that Rocco was stuffing into a small furnace—identical except it wasn't pressed. Helen ironed all of Jake's work clothes because as she put it, "You're a workingman, not a friggin bum." Jake gulped the red fluid in the water tumbler. The home-brewed wine made him feel better. His head started to clear a bit, and the world started to slow down. He put on a pair of denim trousers as Rocco was burning the ones he had worn.

"These fit pretty good, Rocco. What are ya doing with clothes my size?"

"I'ma fixin you upa, Mista Jake, nonja worry."

Rocco had taken on a new image to Jake. He was no longer that little Guinea from the wine joint. He'd been through this before.

CHAPTER 11

J ake saw the large truck pulling away from the rear of the hall. He didn't recognize the driver, but from the dark complexion, he figured he must be a Sicilian.

"Where's Dooley, Rocco?"

"He's on the way to the hospital, nonja worry."

Jake glanced at the regulator clock in the mahogany frame over Rocco's counter.

"Five to nine. What about the mess in the hall?"

"It's a cleaned upa."

"What about the car out front?"

"The policia should have thata car by now."

"Rocco, please tell me what in the hell is going on!"

"You goa to the hall, Mista Jake. I speak to you later." Rocco held out a heavy checkered jacket to Jake to replace the one that he had burned in the furnace. "Justa you act lika nothing hasa happened. I speaka to you later."

Jake took a large swallow of the potent Guinea Red and walked over to the hall. Pat McGinty was standing in Dooley's office as Jake apprehensively approached.

"Where's Dooley?"

"I don't know. It's not like him to be late."

The assistant handed Jake the work order for the day, and he casually glanced at it. He looked around the room but was unable to find anything that would betray what he had done.

"Look's pretty good. They even cleaned the window. You can see out now."

Jake's head snapped when McGinty spoke. "Who cleaned what?"

"I don't know. Dooley was always saying he was gonna have the place cleaned. I guess he did. Musta had it done last night. I can still smell the pine oil they used. Hey, Jake, you don't look so good. Anything wrong?"

"Nah, I had a rough night. I just don't bounce back like I used to."

"Yeah, I know. Me too," McGinty agreed.

They slid back the large doors, and the gang bosses went to their unofficial areas and climbed onto the foot-worn packing crates to start the morning shape-up. After the allotted men had been picked, the gang bosses huddled together. Jake glanced around and spotted a group of about twenty-five men off to one side. They were the Jersey men. No one had hired them. They all seemed to be talking at once. Every one of them was gesturing emphatically with their hands.

Friggin Guineas! he thought. Then he remembered Rocco. *Well, I suppose there are some good ones.*

CHAPTER 12

Jake was walking to pier 10 from the hall when he saw the black Ford glide to a stop at the curb. Detective Gross was on the sidewalk, taking those long strides of his and corning directly at Jake.

Don't panic. Don't run. It was self-defense. You didn't kill on purpose. Act natural…

"Morning, Jake. How you doing? Look, I've got some unpleasant business with you. Can we go into Dooley's office?"

Before he had a chance to speak, the policeman had his large hand on Jake's shoulder and was guiding him toward the office. It was the last place Jake wanted to be, especially with a cop.

Gross was good, but not this good. How the hell could he know? It was only ten o'clock. How the hell did he know?

"You don't look so good, Jake. Feelin' lousy, huh? Had a rough night, didn't you?"

Again, before he could answer, Gross began chewing on his large green cigar, working it from one side of his mouth to the other as he talked. Jake never noticed before, but now that he was looking straight at him, it was quite a disgusting habit.

Light the friggin' thing! That pine oil smell is enough to knock your hat off. Keep calm, his inner self urged.

"Gross, you got an extra cigar?"

"I thought you had a rough night, Jake?"

"I did, but this is a sure cure. It'll either—"

"Yeah, I know, *kill* or cure you."

Why did be put the emphasis on kill, or is it my imagination? Jake was seated opposite Gross, who was puffing on the cigar and flicking the ashes under the desk.

"Who cleaned up the place? Looks pretty good. I love that pine oil smell, don't you? Well, anyway, Jake, I guess you're curious as to what's up." Again, before he could speak, Gross continued on, "Dooley's been hurt. He's in Lutheran Hospital with a possible fractured skull. We got some half-assed witness in the car. The car's been reported stolen for four days now. Dooley doesn't know a thing. He just keeps askin' for you."

"What happened, Eddie? Is he gonna die?"

"No, no. He was crossing Third Avenue, according to this witness, when this black LaSalle came out of nowhere and slammed into Dooley then into a light pole. He describes the driver as a colored guy who just jumped out and ran up toward Fourth Avenue. Probably got on the subway."

"Who's the witness?"

"Some greaseball—real dark, looks colored himself."

Everything was falling into place. Rocco's helper must have driven the car at the pole and jumped out before it hit. Then they took Dooley out of the truck and placed him on the street while everyone was going to the car. The truck then left with the rest of the cargo.

Boy, do I owe Rocco a debt. Finally, he spoke out loud. "Any other witnesses, Ed?"

"Nah, you know this neighborhood, Jake: 'I don't know nuttin'.'" Gross did a good imitation of the way the area residents cooperated with the police. "I was lucky to turn up this greaseball. We'll never find the driver, but Dooley might have seen something that could help us. So if he tells you anything, let me know, okay? Okay, thanks, Jake. I'm sorry I had to tell you about Jim, but he is asking for you. The docs say his insides are busted up and his skull might be fractured, but they think they can piece him together. Well, so long, Jake. I'll see you around. Ya know, this place looks pretty good when it's clean. So long."

Jake took the cigar from his mouth and threw it on the floor. His hands were shaking. He made his way out of the office to the knot of gang bosses who were practically bursting with curiosity. He repeated to them exactly what Detective Gross had told him. They all agreed what a no-good bastard the driver of the car was. Poor old Jim Dooley, he was all right even if he did slip the Jersey men in before their own.

"I wonder if his son knows. I wonder if they got him a priest." McGinty spoke to everyone in general and no one in particular. "I'll call the hospital and tell them to get him a priest. He might want to go to confession."

Jake thought quickly, *Holy shit, I never thought of that. One of those nosy Protestant witches would probably listen, and Dooley might tell the priest what he saw!*

"No, no, don't!" The words came out much louder than he had intended. All eyes were looking at Jake. It was McGinty who finally spoke. "What's the matter, Jake? Why not? Who the hell are you to say no?"

"I mean, er, Gross told me. Er, he assured me that Dooley is gonna be okay. I mean, he, a priest, might just scare him." He felt himself flush. He was starting to crumble. The pressure had finally gotten to him. *God, don't let them notice.*

"I'm going to go up there now, and I'll ask him. How's that?"

The pier bosses all nodded in agreement, and McGinty told Jake that he'd cover him so he wouldn't have to hurry back.

CHAPTER 13

"I'm Jake Ryan."

"Oh yes, Mr. Ryan. Mr. Dooley's been asking for you. Please come this way."

As Jake followed the young nurse down the corridor, his thoughts went to Helen and the girls. *What if I get arrested? I can see the neighborhood kids teasing my girls: "You're father's a murderer in jail!" Kids are vicious bastards.*

"Here we are, Mr. Ryan. Now please don't stay long. He needs his rest. Mr. Ryan, do you feel all right?"

"Huh? Oh er, yes, Nurse, I'm fine. Thank you."

Once inside the room, Jake went directly to the bed. With tubes in his arms and up his nostrils, added to by the discoloration on his face, Old Dooley was a pretty sad sight.

Jake, bending low, spoke, "Jim, Jim, it's me—Jake."

"Ah, Jake," Dooley rasped. "Jake, thank you, thank you!"

"Jim, what's it all about? What was going on?"

"It's a long story, Jake, a long story. Gross was here and told me I'd been hit by a car. I didn't have a chance to get any of the details. I didn't tell him anything, Jake. Don't worry. I didn't speak at all." It was becoming increasingly harder and harder for Jake to understand Dooley. The medication was taking effect. The young nurse stepped into the room and, with a hissing sound, beckoned Jake outside. He didn't want to leave, but he realized he wasn't going to get any answers from the old man today.

CHAPTER 14

W alking back to the piers, Jake saw a green-and-white police car cruising along Fourth Avenue. He'd never been afraid of the police. Quite the contrary. He'd always gotten along exceptionally well with them. At the sight of the cruiser car, he found himself looking for a place to hide. He fought the tremendous urge to run. He saw the barroom door and headed toward it. Once inside, he felt safe. It was a kind of sanctuary for him. After five fast jiggers of Scotch, he felt better.

Those cops aren't after me. Gross would have taken me in if they knew anything. I'm clear. It was self-defense. His thoughts became jumbled bits and pieces of the morning. His watch told him it was eleven thirty. He placed it to his ear and could hear it ticking. *Holy shit, it's still morning!* Time seemed to be standing still for him.

"Ya want another one, Mac?" the barkeep asked.

"Yeah, and make it a double. I'm in a hurry."

"In a hurry to do what?"

"To get loaded. Now just pour and mind your own business."

Helen opened the door. "Where'd you find him, McGinty?"

"Now look, Helen, I wasn't with him. Don't go blaming me for this."

"McGinty, you donkey son of a bitch, where'd you find him?"

"He was in Johnny Red's on Marginal and Twenty-Ninth Street. I had the boys out looking for him all day. I wasn't with him."

Helen's temper was famous on the waterfront. When Jake would get a load on, one of the men would get him to his front door, and Helen invariably would turn her wrath on the Good Samaritan, mainly because Jake would be "too friggin polluted to hear me."

"All right, McGinty, bring him here. Girls, go into the parlor." She never liked the girls to see Jake drunk. She knew the older ones were starting to realize what was going on, but she wanted to keep it from them as long as she could. Jake could barely walk. Middie had one arm and McGinty the other as they got him to the bedroom door.

Helen opened the door and dismissed McGinty. "I can take it from here. Thanks a lot."

McGinty was just as happy to leave. The prospect of an encounter with Helen Ryan was one thing he did not relish.

"Middie, I love ya. Ya know I really do. You're wunnerful. I love ya and the girls too. Where are my girls? Girls! Oh, girls, Daddy's home."

"Shut up, ya big bastard! They'll learn soon enough what a friggin disgrace they have for a father. Now get into bed. Look at you! I iron your clothes, and you come home all mussed." At that point, Helen punched Jake in the forehead with a clenched fist. She knocked him right on to the bed, and there he lay with a smile on his face, sleeping the sleep of a baby. She took his work boots off and then covered him with the extra blanket. Before leaving the room, she removed all his money from his wallet and pockets.

As Jake put it, "She rolled me." Helen bent over him and gave him a kiss. She turned out the light and left him.to his drunken dreams.

The Big Ben alarm clock abruptly broke the morning silence. Helen stirred as she reached out to the night table to silence the piercing sound. Sensing he was gone, she turned to find her intuition had not failed her. It was six thirty and still dark. Where could he have gone? This was different from the other times he'd gone out on a tear.

Something was on his mind. He would always confide in her when something was going on. All these thoughts crossed her mind as she began preparing for the day ahead.

CHAPTER 15

Jake, with the help of some glib talk, persuaded the nurse on duty to let him in to see Dooley. He shook him softly, trying to rouse him from his sleep.

"Jake, Jake, what time is it, lad?"

"About 6:00 a.m., Jim. How do you feel?"

"Lousy."

"The nurse says you're going to be fine, Jim. You just have to take it easy. I really hate to do this to you, but I've got to know. What was going on? What'd I get into?"

Dooley began speaking in a very labored manner. "Jake, I have to swear you to secrecy. Swear by the saints you'll not divulge what I tell you. Swear it, Jake." The old man grabbed Jake by the arm and held it in a viselike hold.

"I swear it, Jim. I swear it."

"Years ago I fell in love, Jake. She was beautiful—long black hair, green eyes, teeth and skin as white as milk. I loved her, and she loved me. My Kathleen was my life. Her parents were against us because of our ages. I was nineteen, and she was only seventeen. This was long before you were born, Jake. This was forty-five years ago. It seems like yesterday.

"We were so deeply in love. You'll have to understand. She was a good girl, Jake, and our nights of courting were pure and clean. As pure as she was. You're from this country, Jake. You don't know what it's like in the small villages of the old country. People were mean and vicious. They began to gossip about us. At first it was whispered, but when it became obvious what they were saying about us, I decided the best thing would be for me to go to England and work on the docks until Kathleen's parents would give us permission to marry."

The old man's eyes started to water as he recalled the parting between himself and the lovely Kathleen almost half a century ago.

"'Twas a lovely night. There was a lake at the end of the village. I got there early and tried to think out how I'd tell her I was leaving. Suddenly, I looked up, and she was standing there—a vision, Jake. Ah, I can still see her, the moon glistening on her hair. Jake, I loved her so much!"

The old man was crying unashamedly, and Jake began to feel uneasy. Dooley finally dried his eyes and continued his narration.

"I tried, but I just couldn't find the words. We made pure love to each other. It was the truest act of love that had ever taken place. Her bridal bed was made of shamrocks and wild flowers, the kind that you'll only find in the old country during the spring. The minutes became hours, and with each passing second, our love was pledged over and over again. She knew I was troubled, yet she never let on. She never asked or pried. She put her complete faith in me, Jake. Near daylight, I left her at her cottage fence. She looked.me full in the face and told me not to worry, to do what I felt was right. She said she'd understand. I started to tell her my plans, but she placed her hands on my lips and just repeated her love for me and her faith in me. She turned and ran to the cottage.

"I left for England a few hours later. I wrote to her every day I was working on the docks and living with some distant cousins. I never got any answers from her. I found out later that her parents intercepted all my letters and burned them. They felt I had shamed them. You see, Jake, Kathleen was with child. I had a friend from the village who came to England for work. I ran into him, and he told me of Kathleen and her family's treatment of her, for by now it was common knowledge. I booked passage on the first available ship home. I was too late. Too late to even see her, Jake. Too late to tell her I loved her. She was dead. They wouldn't even bury her in the church. They said she was a fallen woman. Her own family turned her out. My grandmother took her in. She delivered the baby for her, nursed her, did all she could to save her, but Kathleen had lost her will to live. She didn't doubt my love, but she had given up hope of seeing me ever again."

"I took the infant, and with borrowed money, I booked passage to the US of A. I got a job sweeping out a saloon on the waterfront in Manhattan. The owner felt sorry for me and my son, so he let me have a room in the back. T'wasn't easy for the young lad, but he survived, and I survived. Finally I came to Brooklyn, changed my name and the lad's too. I was working steady on the piers and was home every night. I paid a woman to watch the boy when I was working. One day I went to a priest's house in New York on a pretext of some sort or another and stole a baptismal certificate. I filled it in. So began my son's new identity. You know, Jake, in those days a baptism certificate was as valid as a birth certificate. Record keeping wasn't like it is today."

CHAPTER 16

Jake nodded his understanding and gave Dooley a sip from the water glass on the nightstand. Dooley finished and sank deeply into the pillows. Jake felt terrible for making the old man tell the sad tale, but he had to get the reasons for the three killings straight in his mind.

"Jake, crank up the bed a bit, if you'd be so kind."

"Sure, Jim."

"Thank you, Jake."

"Jim, I hate to put you through all this but—"

Dooley held up a hand to silence Jake. "I owe it to you, lad. It's the least I can do for you." Dooley continued, "And so, Jake, the years passed. I kept getting better jobs on the piers, more responsibility, more money. The lad kept getting older, and his school grades were better than the other kids'. The lad was bright. He was a good athlete, and he even got jobs after school. Our life was good, Jake. I felt proud. Out of nothing, I had built a new and good way of life. The boy thinks his mother died about a year after his birth. He thinks he's American born. Well, all this is ancient history, but somehow or other, Grasso and his two cronies found out the real story and were using it to force me to put the Jersey men on the shifts.

"Jake, for the life of me, I don't know how they found out. It's killing me! Of course, they didn't have the full story. All they knew was that my name isn't Dooley. They know I'm not a citizen, and that there's no record of my son's birth or his mother's death. It was enough to make me do as they asked. I couldn't let them go poking around. I didn't know what they'd find out. You can't fault me for it, Jake. You'd have done the same thing." Dooley was starting to raise his voice, and his face was starting to flush. Jake placed a gentle hand on his shoulder, and it seemed to have a calming effect on the white-haired man.

"Yesterday they came to me and told me they wanted the Jersey men on the *Liberty Queen*."

"You mean the one with all the ammunition on board?"

"Yes, the very one! Now, I'd heard about the Germans offering big money if you'd just place a package on the ship, but I really didn't believe it—not till yesterday, anyway. Those lousy mutts were going to sabotage that ship, Jake. They threatened me with everything. I knew they wouldn't kill me 'cause they needed me, but then One Ear said he was going to go to the bishop and tell him my boy lied, tell him my son was illegitimate. Jake, do you know what that would mean?"

"No, Jim, I don't. So what if you weren't married?"

"Jake, you can't be a priest if your parents aren't married. The boy doesn't know, and he's up for monsignor now. The scandal would ruin him!"

CHAPTER 17

So now all the pieces fit. Jake sat back in the chair. *That's what it was all about. Those lousy rotten-bum bastards! They'd stoop that low! They'd blow up a ship with supplies our boys need. They'd destroy an old man's life for money!* He was glad he'd killed them. He felt good inside. He knew from that moment on that he'd never regret his actions. He looked out the hospital room window and saw the sun shining brilliantly in the early morning sky. A new day. A good day.

"Jim, I want you to know I'll never breathe a word of this to another living soul. I'll take this to the grave with me. God bless you, Jim."

"God be with you, Jake. God be with you."

The walk back to the piers was a pleasure for Jake. The streets seemed clean somehow. The people that were scurrying from their homes to the subways all seemed to be smiling and waving to one another.

Odd, he thought, *I never really thought of it before, but people are friendly.*

Before he realized it, his long legs had taken him to Rocco's place. He entered, and Rocco greeted him as if nothing had taken place.

"Hey, Mista Jake, howa you thisa morning?"

"Rocco, about yesterday, I just wanted to—"

'Hey, Mista Jake, have a drink. Lika you say, to warda offa the morning chill."

Jake accepted the shot glass and tried to thank Rocco again, but it was to no avail. Obviously, Rocco didn't want to be thanked or have the matter rehashed. So Jake respected his wishes and drank his drink.

About four days later, a small article in the *Daily Mirror* caused a minor stir along the waterfront:

> Police on Staten Island have discovered the bodies of Louis Grasso and Tony Mastrion and another man as yet unidentified. The men were found buried in a shallow grave about one hundred yards from the South Beach Trolley Car Barn. Children playing in the vicinity observed what appeared to be a hand protruding from the sand and notified police. Patrolman James Touhey and Edward Carey responded and made the grim find. Detectives investigating the case feel it was a gangland slaying, as Grass and Mastrion had police records and were known to be affiliated with the underworld. Mastrion was bludgeoned to death, Grasso was stabbed, and the unidentified man was strangled to death. Police say it's the classic example of how the underworld rids itself of those who have failed to live up to the gangland code.

The day the story was published, there was little weeping about "society's loss." The men who owed money to Grasso were relieved because they knew all his records were kept in his head. Also, he was alone in the moneylending enterprise. Therefore, they wouldn't be forced to pay the exorbitant interest on loans they had made from him. Jake agreed that "it was about time." They really must have stepped on someone's toes.

Those Guineas are really something. I mean, you'd think they'd shoot them or something. What a way to go!

CHAPTER 18

Helen had a fierce look in her eyes as I walked into the Candy Store one morning. Jake was still sleeping, and you could feel the tension.

"Morning, Helen."

But instead of the usual cordial and sincere greeting, a curt nod was the response. I took a copy of *The News* and perched on the leather-covered swivel stool. Then I saw Mona. She was seated in Helen's armchair, with her daughter, Cheryl, lying on the card table. The table was used by Jake as a TV stand. Helen's chair was reserved for special company and for herself. Mona didn't fit into the special company category at all.

She was about thirty-eight years old, was flat chested, and had four teeth in her head—two on the top right and two on the bottom left. It was very easy to understand why she had lost her teeth. The ones she had left were covered with tar and moss and brown decay spots. Her clothing befitted her facial appearance. She was dirty right down to her toenails. To hear her tell it, she was the Mother of the Year, but her actions belied her statements. She was of Arabic extraction, and Jake constantly called her Camel Jockey, which evoked a stream of four-letter words that even made Jake quiver.

"Cheryl, you lousy little bitch—"

"Hold it, Mona," Helen interrupted just in time. "This is a place of business, not a house of ill repute. That kid is only fourteen months old. Now, if you're gonna call her that, don't do it in here. In my store. Get your dirty little ass outa my chair and that kid off my table. You're not gonna use that language around here again. You're a nervy bastard, and I've let you slide long enough. Now, get outa here before I throw you out myself."

43

Mona was speechless. This was a rare feat to accomplish, but Helen had done it, all right. Mona scooped up her Cheryl and the child's soiled clothing and, without looking left or right, made a hasty exit out onto Third Avenue.

I was the first to speak. "Helen, you are remarkable. She's had that coming for a long time. I know that if I had said anything to her, she'd have turned on me with every curse word she knew."

"If she dares to say anything to me, I'd give her a fast puck into her mouth, and she knows damn well I would." Helen had gone back to her usual self almost as soon as Mona was out the door. "Ya know, the thing is, that baby is cute, and if that diz bang keeps calling her all those fancy names, God knows how she'll turn out. There's a way of cursing at kids so they know you love them. But the way that slob does it, it comes out sounding like hate."

"I know what you mean, Helen. I really do."

CHAPTER 19

The sign in the store window spoke for itself: "Closed. Jake's drunk again."

Whenever Jake would "break out and go on a friggin bat," Helen would do all the chores at the store until she ran out of patience, and then the sign went in the window. But before the locks on the heavy protective metal gate were snapped into place, the events didn't vary much.

"I swear, as soon as he gets that pension check from the docks, I'm gonna throw him out."

"Why are you going to wait? How come you don't do it now?" I asked.

"I couldn't throw him out broke. That wouldn't be fair. I mean, after all, he has supported us all these years. But I swear, I'll throw the bum out. He can come around once a week, and I'll give him a meal and some money. But whatever he does after that is up to him. I don't give a damn if he drinks, but he won't eat anything. Then he flounders around behind the counter and insults all the customers. Look at him over there."

I looked over at Jake as he was stumbling toward the little icebox. As he opened it, I could see it was crammed full of beer. He removed one, opened it, took a long drink, and smacked his lips together. "Ah, that's good. I needed that."

He wobbled back behind the counter. Helen continued to talk about Jake as if he wasn't there. Finally he said, "Ya know, this is like being at your own wake. People talk about the poor dead bastard as if he can't hear them. Well, I got news for you. When I really go, you better say nice things about me, or I'll come back to haunt you all."

Helen rolled her eyes heavenward and let out a sigh. Jake had snuck up next to her and shouted, "Boo! I'm a ghost." She jumped from the chair, frightened by the sound. Jake started to laugh. Helen, not thinking it too funny, picked up the nearest thing she could reach and threw a three-quarter full can of beer at Jake. It hit him in the chest and soaked the front of his shirt. He still stood there, laughing, as she threw up her arms in a sign of defeat.

CHAPTER 20

Jake had finished for the day, and he and Wally Thatcher, his friend of over twenty years, were settling down on two stools in McCarthy's. Old Dan McCarthy was dead now, and his son had sold to two retired pier bosses. The new owners knew Dan and decided to keep the name as a sort of tribute to his memory. Jake's mood had been sullen. Usually, Wally could get a smile out of him. But today, all he got for his efforts was a grunt.

Wally, unlike Jake, was unmarried and loved to go to Jake's home to soak up the family atmosphere. The girls all called him Uncle Wally, and he'd play endlessly with them, throwing them in the air, letting them blindfold him, and listening to them squealing as he feigned stumbling into the furniture. He was shorter than Jake but built as powerfully. His only physical drawback was a pronounced limp. As a child, he had contracted infantile paralysis. He came out of the encounter with only the limp. He considered himself lucky to be able to get around as well as he could. His work on the piers was so good that he was made pier boss when Jim Dooley retired. That was almost a full year ago. His new position hadn't changed him at all, and the men still liked and respected him as they did before his promotion.

Every Sunday, Jake said, "For Christ's sake, Middie, don't bring any of those dizzy old maids around here anymore. Wally's a friend. If he ever hooked up with any of those man-hungry spinsters, he'd never speak to us again."

"Is that true, Wally? Is that what you think I'm doing? Do you think I'm trying to match you up with one of my girlfriends?"

He just stood there and smiled at Helen. "I know I'll never find anyone as wonderful as you, Middie, so there's no use in my settling for someone less than 100 percent. If this big bum is ever mean to you, just let me know. I'll take you and the girls with no questions asked."

"You hear that, Jake? You better be nice to me."

"What the hell is eating you, Jake? I've been breaking my back all day, trying to snap you out of your mood. Now, what's eating you?"

"Aw, you wouldn't understand, Wally."

"Try me."

"You and I have been friends almost all our lives, Wally, but I don't know if you'd understand." They both took long swallows from the glasses in front of them, and Jake continued, "I have a pretty good life here. I mean, Middie and the kids are doing all right. I work steady. I don't really work hard. I have some money in the bank. I'm not really breaking my ass at all." Before Wally could answer, Jake started to speak again.

"You see, Wally, I've never contributed to this country at all. I've never had a chance to say thanks to America for…well, for taking my parents in from the old country, for giving me a high school education, for letting me do as I please. Wally, if I don't take this opportunity, I'll never forgive myself. You see, the ships are coming back with casualties on them. They may be boys in age, but they're men in my eyes—more than I'll ever be. Can you understand this at all? I've got to be a part of this war. I've got to do something for my country."

"I've tried to get into it myself, Jake. I've been turned down by everyone, including the air raid wardens, because of this bum leg. Yes, I can understand, but your problem is Middie."

"That's right. I don't know how to tell her. How will she get along when I'm gone?"

"Jake, why don't you go home and explain it to her just the way you did to me? I know Middie, and I know she'd be proud of you and would be the first to tell you to go and do what you feel is right for yourself and your family's future."

"You think so, Wally? You really do?"

"I know so, Jake. Besides, I'll be here if she or the girls need anything. At least that way I'll be able to feel that I've contributed to the war effort. Even if Uncle Sam can't use me, maybe the Ryans can."

"Where is the hell is Fort Riley? Kansas?"

"In Kansas, Middie. Mid, are you and the girls gonna be all right? It's too late now to back out, but level with me."

"Listen, ya big lug, haven't I always gone along with you? I've fought you a few times, but you know I'm with you. Sure, I've thrown a few things around in our time, but you know that if I wanted to, I could have hit you without any problem. Jake, I love you. Not like you see in the movies. I love you with my heart." Jake started to speak, but Helen continued, "You've given me and the girls a wonderful life. Sure, you've been drunk more times than I care to remember, but you've been faithful to me, and that's what makes me know you love me the way I love you."

Jake drew Helen close to him and breathed a deep sigh. "Middie."

"Yes?"

"Nothing, just Middie."

The memory of that moment and the following night of love would be recalled many times by both Middie and Jake in the months of loneliness and trial to follow.

CHAPTER 21

"O'Leary."

"Yo."

"Edwards."

"Yo."

"McDermott."

"Here."

"Sprague."

"Yo."

"McKee."

"Yo."

"Fox."

"Yo."

"Connelly."

"Here."

"Freck."

"Present."

"Third Squad present and accounted for, sir."

"Very good, Sergeant Ryan. Carry on with the orders of the day."

"Yes, sir."

During basic training, Jake had taken a battery of exams and was found eligible for the officers' training, affectionately known as the ninety-day wonder course. He was debating whether or not to go to the course when the Army made the decision for him. He was notified to report to the base commander's office at 0730 hours one frosty morning. It was all very cordial, but the crux of the matter was that he didn't have any college background, plus his age. "After all, there are Captains and Majors younger than you," he'd been told.

Also to be taken into consideration was his family. The life expectancy of a second lieutenant in combat was ninety seconds if he was in the first assault wave. Feeling slightly dejected, Jake left the office to return to his duties. It could have been nice, but...aw, who cared? They had made him a sergeant, hadn't they? As long as he could get into the action. As long as he could satisfy this overwhelming desire to do something for his country.

The orders came. He had been assigned to the 101 Airborne Division. Although his age had almost kept him out, he knocked on every door he could, and just to stop him from going to General Eisenhower himself, he finally got to Fort Benning, Georgia, and jump school. The training was rigorous, but he was in top physical condition. His platoon marveled at his capacity for calisthenics. Kids nineteen were dropping by the dusty Georgia roadsides, while he was still going strong. He knew this was the life for him.

The letters from Middie were filled with good news from home: the girls were fine, Uncle Leif was arrested for a fight in a bar, Jim Dooley's son was being considered for bishop of Brooklyn, Wally still came over for Sunday dinner...

Everyone was real proud of him. The allotment checks were coming, so money wasn't that much of a problem. They all sent their love.

He loved her letters. They were filled with information that he could care less about, but the way she wrote was just the way she spoke, and that almost made him not miss her as much as he did. He hadn't been home in four months. He still had another four weeks to finish parachute school, then a thirty-day furlough. Holy damn! Thirty days at home. That would be nice. Thirty days, then overseas. He wouldn't tell her that. Not until he had to. He knew she was worried, but he also knew that she was tough.

CHAPTER 22

The weeks of practice were finally over. The large wooden scaffold they had been using to jump from, which simulated a plane jump, was to be replaced by a jump from a real plane.

The engine roared until it was almost too much for ears to bear. The ground started to pass swiftly at eye blurring speed. One man started to gag and cough. The first sergeant abruptly jerked the man's head toward the ceiling and, in a voice that drowned out the motor's roar, shouted to the men, "All heads immediately look toward the plane's ceiling!" Each man remembered the admonition of the jump master. "You people will not, I repeat, will not look out of the windows or at the floor. You will, I repeat, you will look at the ceiling of this aircraft. Any man who deviates from this routine will, I repeat, will face me if and when he survives the first jump."

Jake unbuckled the seat belt and adjusted the parachute harness straps. He, for the first time since he volunteered for the airborne outfit, had a touch of regret. He couldn't shake the feeling. It was just something inside him that mad him feel uneasy. The orange light started to flash, and as if controlled by a master puppeteer, forty-two men rose wordlessly together. Each man adjusted the back parachute of the man in front. The first sergeant gave the order to hook up. The troopers responded by attaching their static line to a thin wire that ran the length of the plane.

"Stand in the door." The first man walked woodenly toward the open hatch. The air rushing in was frigid and thin. He didn't know about the others, but Jake thought he was going to pass out. He was sure it was because of the rarified atmosphere and not out of fear.

The green light flashed on, and the jump master tapped the young soldier, who then stepped out of the plane. All eyes were on the young trooper as his chute billowed opened in the bright-blue November sky. A feeling of relief swept over everyone as the next man and then the next stepped into the yawning cavity in the plane's side.

Three more to go, Ryan. Don't lose your nerve. You wanted this, you stupid bastard. Now you got it. One more and you go. Jake shut off the dialogue he was having with himself and strained to remember the procedure he'd been taught in case the static line didn't pull open the main chute. His mind was blank. All he could think of was being hit by the tail wing of the plane. He'd never given that any thought before. Why now?

The chute opened with a jerk, and he opened his eyes. The earth below looked like the patchwork quilt Helen had made just before the twins were born. He looked up and saw the white billow above his head. He marveled at the feeling. The air smelled clean and tasted good to him. He didn't know how air could be tasted, but he felt sure he was swallowing large chunks of tasty air. He hit the ground with his knees slightly bent and rolled exactly the way he'd been practicing all those lonely weeks. His first jump was finished. He loved it. He knew he hadn't made a mistake by cajoling his way into the airborne. This is where the action is!

CHAPTER 23

"Wake up, buddy. You can't stay here. We gotta clean up."
Jake collected himself and realized he was in the Grand Central Station.

Holy shit, I'm in New York. I'm home!

He hoisted the heavy olive-green barracks bag onto his shoulder in one motion. He'd lost some weight but was more solid now than at any time in his life. He felt good. He looked good in his uniform. He was proud of the insignia sown onto his sleeve: the screaming eagle. The jump boots he wore were polished to the highest gloss the black leather could produce. Yes, Jake was home, feeling good and feeling proud. He left the lower level and made his way through the thousands of people meeting returning GIs and others seeing them off. On the terminal level, he stepped at the circular marble information desk and looked up at the large oval bronze-colored clock. It was eleven thirty. Too late to call Helen; she'd probably be asleep by now. The girls had school in the morning. He hadn't written to tell her when he'd be home. A surprise would be better.

With very long strides, he climbed the well-traveled stairs leading to Vanderbilt Avenue, carefully guiding the barracks bag so as not to bump any passerby.

He hit Vanderbilt Avenue and found it was snowing lightly. When he left Georgia, it was unseasonably warm. Jake had buried his heavy OD overcoat in the bottom of the bag. The last thing he wanted was to catch a cold and be laid up for his furlough. The cab stand on the street had two dodge-checker cabs sitting there. Jake opened the rear door, and the cabbie asked where he was going.

"Listen, Mac, if it's Brooklyn or Queens, you're outa luck. I mean, we all got orders to stay around the city. You know how it is."

Oh well, New York hasn't changed. Jake should have realized it. He decided to walk to B'way instead of going back into the terminal and taking the shuttle to Times Square.

The six long blocks were still busy with people going here and there as the tall soldier weaved his way in and out of the pedestrians and entered the subway at Times Square for the half-hour ride on the Sea Beach Express. Ah, it was good to be home. He couldn't wait to see Middie and the girls. The snow was starting to stick, covering Fourth Avenue with a nice, clean white blanket. He used to hate snow and rain when he worked the waterfront, but now, well, it did make things kind of pretty. He walked past the Stein House and saw Eddie Corbin, the friendly bartender, passing the time with some of the regulars. The Irish Haven on the next corner was empty except for one old-timer sleeping at the end of the bar. His pace quickened as he turned into Fifty-Sixth Street up toward Fifth Avenue.

"Hi, Jake!"

Jake peered through the now heavily falling snow but couldn't make out the face in the dark auto.

"Hop in. I'll drive you down to the Precinct. What a homecoming! I guess you're a little pissed off."

Jake knew, by the manner of speaking, that it was Eddie Gross. "Hello, Ed. Pissed off about what?"

"The arrest."

Jake's heart thumped so hard he thought that Gross and his partner could hear it. His mind went swiftly back to that day in Dooley's office…

Gross continued, "You and I both know it can be straightened out. So here's what I want you to do. Get in, Jake. You'll catch your death."

Automatically, Jake climbed into the rear seat of the cruiser car. *That friggin cigar—I wonder if he sleeps with one in his mouth.*

Gross continued, "Now, you go into the precinct and tell the desk officer you want to press charges against the owner and the bartender for assault."

"Hold it! Hold it! What the hell are you talking about?"

"Helen, of course. Didn't you know?" Without waiting for an answer, he continued, "There was a shower tonight for Dotty Smith. For some reason, they held it in the back room of Artie Kay's joint. Well, the bartender, Willie Nelson, started, as usual, passing comments toward all the girls. Artie made an advance toward Helen."

"What kind of an advance?"

"Well, he grabbed her tit, and she hit him in the head with a full quart of Canadian. Nice shot, too, seventeen stitches. He looks like a swami."

"How's Helen?"

"She's fine. A little loaded, but fine."

"What about Nelson?"

"Oh, you know him, a real shithead. He made the mistake of pushing Helen. So her sister Maisie clouted him with a chair and opened him up."

"Who called the cops?"

"Well, that's another story," Gross continued. "This as asshole rookie, Thomas J. Flaherty by name, has the foot post, sees Nelson getting clouted, runs in with his gun out, and lines them up against the wall. I mean, with his gun out. Anyway, there's the bride-to-be, her mother, her eighty-year-old grandmother, Helen, Maisie, and the rest of 'em up against the wall with their hands up, and stupid with his gun in his hand. He tried to get someone at the bar to call for a wagon, but they all refused. This guy is really stupid, Jake. If it were men fighting, he wouldn't even have gone into the joint."

Gross's partner interrupted, "Eddie, he is a coward. He's not stupid. He's just a coward."

"Anyway, Jake, Helen turns away from him, goes to the phone, and calls for a wagon. Then while he's sputtering, she opened the side door and let everyone out while she stood in front of the gun. So the windup is that she and Maisie were the only ones that stayed. Willie and Artie are pushing for charges, and Flaherty's fuming. I know once Willy and Artie back off, all he'll want is an apology. Helen will do that for you, right, Jake?"

"Jesus, Ed, I don't know. I sure hope so, but I don't know."

CHAPTER 24

Through some stroke of luck, Jake knew the desk sergeant. He'd gone through elementary school with him, and they'd remained friendly over the intervening years. Middie and Maisie were howling loud and long in another room, but the language was unmistakably Helen's. Willie and Artie were brought before the sergeant, and Jake, acting every inch the concerned husband, demanded loudly that the two injured men be arrested. He shouted that he was going to sue both of them. He'd already gotten a military lawyer, and he was coming over from Fort Hamilton.

"It's a damn shame that a man goes off to war to make the country safe, and his own wife is assaulted—yes, assaulted while her husband isn't around to protect her."

The sergeant behind the desk looked at the two men and, with a straight face, started to castigate the pair. Jake looked at Artie Kay and couldn't help feeling sorry for him. Blood was still oozing through the heavy bandages around his head.

That Helen, she sure could handle herself. I just hope she'll apologize to the rookie and this can be cleared up.

Kay was the first to speak, telling the sergeant it was all a mistake and he and the bartender might have been "a little out of line." If Jake would forget about the arrest and lawsuit, he'd be just as happy to go home and forget about the entire incident. Jake hesitated as the police sergeant started talking.

"Come on now, Mr. Ryan, give the men a break. After all, they're just working men, and their wives would probably kill them if they found out how this whole thing started. So give them a break."

"Yeah, Jake, I'm sorry. It was an accident. You know how it is."

"Well, if you think it's for the best, Sergeant, I'll go along with it, but it better never happen again."

The two casualties from the battle of the bar scurried out into the snow, feeling relieved and slightly embarrassed at what women were able to do to them. One problem remained for Jake, and that was to get Helen to apologize to Flaherty the cop.

"What kind of a guy is this Flaherty fella, Bill?" The sergeant turned his eyes heavenward while muttering an oath, and Jake's spirits sank. "Can't you talk to him? From the way Helen's howling, she's not about to tell him she's sorry."

"Jake, I don't talk about policemen to anyone, but this guy's a real lulu. He's got the nickname of Chowder Head, and the men think he's gutless. I can't figure him out. I'd like to help, but I don't know how."

"Call him out for me, will ya, Bill?"

The sergeant called the cop, and from the rear of the station house, a red-faced, large-headed policeman came toward the desk officer. "You want me, Sergeant Metcalf?" he asked in a nasal tone of voice.

"Yeah, kid, the bartender and the owner changed their minds. They just left. You'll not want to charge the women with anything now, will you, lad?"

Chowderhead. Jake could see how well the name fit as the young officer quoted Helen's transgressions. Jake didn't want to antagonize the cop, but it was funny, and he had all he could to stop from laughing in Chowderhead's face.

Finally, the sergeant interrupted and asked if an apology would make things any easier for him. The young man explained, in the most graphic four-letter words, unequivocally, that he did not wish to see, hear, talk, or listen to Helen or Maisie ever again. Flaherty asked permission to return to his patrol post and to be left alone. Sergeant Metcalf granted permission. After the door closed behind him, Jake and his school-days friend started laughing at the situation and the controlled anger of Patrolman Chowderhead.

CHAPTER 25

He'd been home for three weeks now, and Middie never once asked him where he'd be going when his furlough was over. He knew she was worried, but he figured if he was going overseas, she'd be worried even more. They were having a good time together. After the night in the police station was over, his furlough was just as he wanted it to be. The girls were excited to see him again, and he and Middie had only a few little arguments. All and all, going overseas was the furthest thing on his mind. He just wanted to make things pleasant. He wasn't a fatalist, but he knew his outfit had been trained for combat and his chances were as good as anyone's. He just had the feeling he wouldn't be returning home. He wasn't being dramatic. He just had the feeling.

CHAPTER 26

"Hey, Jake, what's all the excitement?" I entered the store through a knot of adults and youngsters who were milling around the entrance to the Candy Store. "What are the police cars doing here?"

"You know Hilda, the blond who lives up over the store?"

"Yes, what happened?"

"She did the Dutch act."

"She killed herself?" I asked.

"That's right."

"What a shame. I wonder why she'd do a thing like that? I was talking to her yesterday right here."

"Who knows? She was a funny broad. I always knew she was a nut."

"Ya know, Jake, you're a heartless bastard." Helen had just come into the store from the apartment in the back.

"What'd ya mean? I'm not the one who wants to take her color TV."

"Oh bullshit, Jake, I don't want to steal it." Helen turned toward me, looking slightly embarrassed, and started to explain.

"What I said was that I wanted the cops to let me take her color TV to my apartment and if they find her son, I'd ask him if I could buy it from him."

"By the time they find him, the TV will be out of style," Jake interjected. "Tell him what you told the cop about the money."

"Well, he is a stupid bastard—that one is. You know what he did?"

"No," I answered.

"Well, it seems Hilda told one of her coworkers that she was depressed and was going to kill herself. When she didn't show up for work this morning, the girlfriend called the cops. They came in here and asked if I'd seen her or knew if she was home. Anyway, we called on the phone, and the line was out of order. So I told them I'd go upstairs with them—"

"And you're telling me you're not a nosy old witch?"

"Shut up, Jake, and let me finish. Anyway, we go upstairs, I turned the handle on the door, and it swings open. So in we go. Now, you tell me if you think the cop is dopey or not. I stay in the kitchen. One guy goes in the living room, the other to the bedroom. The guy comes from the bedroom, holding a note, and tells his partner to call the sergeant and an ambulance. 'She's dead,' he tells us, 'and she left a note.' Now he tells us that there is a pile of money on the dresser. In the note, Hilda says that the money is for whoever finds her and has the decency to put a sheet over her face. Anyway, the cop did that. Then takes the money into the kitchen and counted it and turned it in. Twelve thousand dollars."

"Mrs. Ryan, I can't see where he was dopey."

"Aw, you're just as bad as Jake. If I had gotten my hands on that money, it never would have made it to the precinct."

"Well, at least you're honest about it."

"Listen, it's no good to her. Her son is a dope fiend, and she has no other relatives. Now, where does that money go? You know the cop isn't gonna get it. It goes to the state. So why not me instead of them? I still say the cop was dopey. You show me a cop that can't use twelve thousand dollars."

"But that's not the point, Mrs. Ryan. It wasn't his."

"Bullshit! She left it for whoever covered up her puss. It's right in the note. I would have taken it."

Jake was winking at me. "You have the nerve to call me I'm a heartless bastard? You're a grave robber. That's what you are." She looked at him and was about to speak when the phone rang.

"Saved by the bell, Jake. You lucked out on that one."

"I guess so. But I would have liked to hear what beauty name she would have called me."

CHAPTER 27

The scene at Grand Central Station was one of complete chaos. Jake and Middie were glad they left the girls home. There must have been thousands of people coming and going, pushing and shoving one another all around the terminal. He didn't want a big scene at the station, but he knew if Middie broke down, he would too. His mother-in-law and Maisie had come with them, and the conversation was light and banal. He had shipped his large barracks bag back to Georgia a week before. While he was home, he wore civilian clothes, so there wasn't any need for all his service gear. He was glad he didn't have to lug the bag around. There were only ten minutes left before train time, so Jake kissed his mother-in-law and Maisie and undiplomatically suggested they go for a cup of coffee in Bickford's and Helen would meet them.

"Jake, you're a terrible bastard. You'll hurt their feelings."

"You couldn't hurt their feelings if you ran over them with a tank. Besides, I have something I want to tell you."

Guiding her through the crowd, Jake found an empty spot near the gate to Track 12. Helen looked at the procession of dark and dirty-looking railroad cars already starting to fill with men in different uniforms, signifying their particular branch of service. Strange how no one was joking or even talking. They all looked the same. They all looked as if they had something on their mind they wanted to tell. Turning to Jake, she looked at him and felt a sudden chill run through her body. His face was set in the same mask as that of the men at the windows of the railroad cars.

"Middie, I want to…if anything…I'm really not too good at this but—"

"Jake, ya big bastard, kiss me."

And he did—a long gentle kiss that both would remember and cherish in the coming period of separation that neither expected to last as long as it did on that winter night in New York City.

CHAPTER 29

"Hello, Helen! Here's another one from Jake."

Helen waved out the second-floor window to Bob Rose, the mailman. Just before he enlisted, Jake had gotten Bob's son-in-law a job on the piers, and in an effort to repay him, he made sure Helen got his letters as early as possible. Bob had already lost a son in the war, and he felt empathy for the families of the men in the service.

Helen started to run through the rooms and was going down the hall stairs when her mother yelled, "Slow down if you want Jake to ever see that kid!" She slowed down to a walk and got to the front door. The spring sun was warm on her face. She felt wonderful and alive. After thanking Mr. Rose and asking after his wife, she raced upstairs to read and reread the long-awaited word from Jake.

All she knew was that he was someplace in England, that the food was good, that the training was still going on, but he couldn't tell her what kind of training he was going through. He was now a staff sergeant, so that meant more money for her and the girls.

Enclosed was a draft for $500 he'd won in a dice game. "That bastard, he'd find a game anywhere. He's a pisser."

She read and reread the letter. The last few lines sort of threw her. It wasn't what he'd written; it was just a feeling.

> So, Mid, don't worry if you don't hear from
> me for a while. With the new rank, I have more
> responsibility and less time to myself. So kiss the
> girls for me, and give your mother a big kick in
> the ass. Love always, Jake.

Mom will get a laugh out of that, she thought. *It's a good thing she knows he's only fooling around.*

"Middie, Middie, what's the matter? You in a daze or something?"

"Oh, hi, Mom. No, I'm all right. I was just reading a letter from Jake. He said to give you his love."

"I'll bet he did! Did you tell him about the baby? You didn't, did you? Middie, you're making a mistake. You better tell him. It's not fair to him or to you. What the hell, Mid! You're the one who's gotta go through everything alone, not him."

"Mother dear, I don't think I'm going to tell him. He's got enough on his mind. Besides, the papers say the war is going well, and our boy might be home sooner than we think."

"Bullshit!" her mother snapped. "You're five months pregnant. He has a right to know and to share it with you."

"Mom, I've decided not to burden him. When it's all over, I'll write and tell him, and we'll both be happy."

Dear Middie, girls, and your mother too.
(I know she'll read this if you leave it lying around.)

Every letter he'd written since he was in England had begun the same way. They were all light and jovial. Two months had passed since she had received the letter she was now rereading for the two hundredth time.

"Why can't he write? Tom O'Brien is in England, and his wife gets a letter at least twice a week. There must be something wrong. I know there's something wrong. The bastard, he'd write if he had to hold the pen with his teeth. He's changed since he went into the Army. His letters proved he'd changed. Why didn't he write?"

The thoughts were going through her mind at a blurring speed. Her instinct told her that Jake wasn't able to write. She knew he would if he was able to, but he couldn't.

CHAPTER 30

She'd just finished mashing the potatoes in the large pot that was dented on one side. She looked at the dent and broke into tears. The girls had never seen their mother crying and didn't know what to do. The twins started crying with fright. Kathleen, now a grown-up girl of eight, told Betsy to get their grandmother. Kathleen was the boss of her sisters. Although only eight, she was advanced for her years and possessed a type of understanding that was beyond her years.

She calmed the twins and walked over to her mother, who was now seated in the living room on the edge of the couch, dabbing at her eyes with the end of her apron.

The child approached the mother and started stroking her hair in the gentle, soothing way Helen had done when one of them had fallen or been hurt by the taunts of their contemporaries.

"He'll be all right, Mommy. He'll be home. God won't let anything happen to him."

Helen looked in wonderment at this child of hers.

How did she know what was wrong? How did she possess the insight at eight years old? She tried to tell Kathleen that she wasn't worried about Jake, but the long-haired little beauty wisely nodded and consoled her by telling her not to worry, that all would be well, and that God would take care of her daddy.

By the time her mother and Betsy came into the room, Helen was composed and on her way into the kitchen.

"What's going on? Are you okay?"

"I'm fine, Mom. I just had a case of the blues. But thanks to little Miss Fix-It, I'm okay now." Helen took a swipe at Kathleen, gently making contact with her rear end. Kathleen responded by letting out a giggly-sounding *ouch*.

"What the hell is going on up here?" the mother asked.

"I was mashing the potatoes, and I looked at the dent in the pot and remembered how it got there. Jake and Leif were out on a tear. Jake finally got home in one of his lovey-dovey drunk moods, and I clobbered him with the pot, cut him above the eye, and put the dent in it. Now I'd be happy if he came in drunk or sober, just so he'd be here."

CHAPTER 31

The last of the schoolchildren had left the Candy Store. Helen was fixing coffee for herself and Jake when the door opened, and three men entered. Each looked like the other—tall with snap brim hats, sunglasses, and cigars.

Helen knew the type.

"Morning! Is there anything I can do for you?"

"Morning, ma'am. I'm Agent McDavitt. This is Agent Gannon and Agent Essex. We're from the FBI."

"Yes."

Each man, in turn, produced a black leather wallet from inside their coats and displayed them to Helen for her inspection. After looking at their credentials with their official pictures and the FBI seal and the signature of the famous director, she nodded her approval.

"I'm Helen Ryan. How about some coffee?"

"Sounds good, ma'am."

All three sat almost in unison. The one doing all the talking (such as it was) reminded her of the detective on television. What was it? Oh yes, "Just the facts, ma'am." She was chuckling to herself at their formal manner when Agent Gannon produced a photo from his pocket and showed it to Helen.

"Mrs. Ryan, do you know this man?"

She looked and immediately recognized George the Bank Robber, as she had labeled the man in the photo. The picture itself was about fifteen years old, but it was George.

"He looks familiar, but I'm not certain. What'd he do?"

"We didn't say he did anything, ma'am. We'd like to talk to him. We understand he lives around the neighborhood."

"Well, I might have seen him—"

The door opened, and in walked Charlie Bennett, the foot patrolman on Third Avenue. A tall man, about forty-five years old, he wore his tailored uniform much the same as a marine wore his blue uniform. Nothing escaped the officer's steel-blue eyes, but the expression didn't betray his knowledge that the three carbon copies were either detectives or federal agents.

"Morning, Helen. How's Jake?"

"Morning, Officer Bennet." She hoped her formal salutation would tip Charlie off to the identity of her customers. But Charlie was a born (as Helen put it) ball-breaker.

"Why so formal? You never called me officer. Morning, gents."

He nodded and sat next to Agent Essex. It could have been the president, but Charlie didn't care.

The three busied themselves finishing their coffee and fishing for dimes to pay for it. Helen was going to tell them to forget it, that it was on the house, but from what she knew about the feds, she felt they might take it the wrong way.

As they were leaving, McDavitt called her to the side and handed her a card with his number on it. "Just in case you see the man in the neighborhood."

"What'd they want?" Jake asked in a strange-sounding voice.

CHAPTER 32

H elen's head turned toward the rear, and she saw Jake standing in the doorway to their apartment.

"Hi, Jake."

"Hi, Charlie. What'd they want, Helen?"

"What's the matter, Jake. You got something to hide?"

Both Charlie and Helen laughed at Helen's question, but Jake's mind went back more than thirty years. *You never know. There is a federal grand jury probe into mafia influences on the waterfront. Who knows how far back they'd go and what they'd find out.*

"They showed me a picture of some guy they want to talk to. They say he's supposed to live in the neighborhood. One of them gave me a number to call if I see him."

"Who is he, Helen?"

Charlie's voice sounded slightly official. "Do you know him?"

"Look, Charlie, I'm not a stool pigeon. If they'd tell me what he did, I'd be more than happy to help. If the guy's a bad guy, that's one thing, but I'm not gonna turn in no friggin guy that didn't pay his taxes."

Charlie started to protest and was going to explain that cooperation was needed with law officers, but he didn't believe what he was going to tell Helen. The agents should have asked him if he knew the man in the photo. Years before, he had had some dealings with the federal people, and he was the only one not to receive any recognition or thanks—at all. He remained inwardly bitter but would never reveal this to the general public.

Jake was stirring his coffee when the portable radio, Charlie had jammed in his pocket, spoke in that metallic voice that only a cop can understand.

"Jake, can I use your phone?"

This was a type of rhetorical question Charlie asked from time to time, knowing the answer would be yes. Jake, as usual, answered, "Yes." After calling the station, Charlie turned to Helen and asked bluntly, "Were they looking for George the Bank Robber?"

Helen looked surprised, and both Jake and Charlie saw it clearly on her face.

"Come on, Middie, tell him what they wanted."

"Listen, Helen, we have a new sergeant in the precinct. He's a real great guy. He's up for an appointment to be a detective boss. The guy deserves it. He's a good boss. They have George positively identified for three robberies in New York City. If the feds take him, they might shoot. If you talk to him, tell him to meet with the sergeant or me and that he won't get hurt. You can do it, Helen. He's gonna get caught anyway, so why not let a friend get him?"

Charlie paused and sipped his coffee. She looked toward Jake, who just turned his back.

"Look, Charlie, he told me he had robbed a bank in Arizona years ago. You know me. I don't even know his last name. I nickname people. I'm not a busybody."

"Holy damn, Middie, you're a pisser! You're the biggest nosy old witch, beside your mother, that I know. You know his name and where he lives. If it's gonna help Charlie or his sergeant and help George, what the hell is the big deal?"

"Shut up, Jake."

"Look, Helen, I'll come back with the sergeant in about fifteen minutes. You think about it, and I'll be back."

CHAPTER 33

Charlie left, and Helen turned to Jake. "I don't know what to do, Jake. Tell me, for Christ's sake."

"If I tell you, you'll do the opposite. I think if you want to help George, give him to the devil you know, not the devil you don't know. Middie, we know Charlie. He is a friend. But he's also a cop. He'll get George, or the feds will get him, and that's all there is to it. But you make up your own mind. I have to take a crap and shave."

An hour later, the door opened. "Helen, this is Sergeant McCarthy."

"Sergeant, this is Mrs. Ryan. Hello, Sergeant. Please call me Helen."

She looked at this giant of a man standing before her. On his chest, over his shield, were rows and rows of different-colored rectangular bars, some with numbers, some with stars on them. Each one designated an award for some act of police bravery or excKathleent action on the part of this young man now seated at her counter. She had the feeling she knew him. His blond hair, closely trimmed, his smooth face…there was something. His eyes—they're so blue. Where had she seen him before?

"You're awfully young to be a sergeant, aren't you?"

"I was lucky, Helen. I happened to hit an exam, and I knew enough answers to barely pass."

"What the frig is wrong with you, Charlie? He looks young enough to be your son. Jake's right. You are a stupid bastard."

The young sergeant looked slightly embarrassed and very amused. Apparently, Charlie was a BB at the store as well as at the station, and Helen thought the sergeant seemed glad to see Charlie have someone give it to him for a change.

The young man finished his coffee and slid twenty cents across the marble counter to Helen. "Well, it's been very nice talking to you, Helen, but I have to get on patrol."

"Wait a minute, Sergeant."

Charlie beckoned Helen to the end of the counter. "Did you decide? I didn't tell him anything. I just told him I wanted him to meet you—you know, for laughs. If he gets George, he's a shoo-in for that detective spot."

"What the frig you gonna get?"

"Nothing, Helen, honest. I just like the kid. You know, he's Irish, and he's a good guy. I'm not fooling."

"What time does he go to lunch?"

"He goes at one o'clock."

"I can't promise anything, Charlie, you know that."

"You're an angel, Helen," Charlie added. "You invite him, he'll feel better."

CHAPTER 34

The neighborhood was flooded with federal agents and detectives from downtown squads. Charlie spotted them as they arrived. The cooperation between federal and city authorities was quite evident. Although it really didn't matter who arrested George, Charlie wanted the police department to make the arrest. More precisely, he wanted the twenty-eight-year-old sergeant to get the recognition for apprehending the desperado.

In reality, George was an old man who drank too much and gambled too much. His wife was dead, he had a daughter living in Arizona, and she wanted no part of him. Helen would make sure that he'd get at least one hot meal a day when he was on a tear. She felt sorry for him.

At one o'clock, Charlie and his youthful superior entered the Candy Store. The sergeant's driver waited around the corner from the store, where Charlie had directed him to stay. Having more than twenty years on the force and being Charlie Bennett, the boss of Third Avenue, this gave him authority over other policemen.

"Hello, Helen, are you sure this isn't an imposition on you? I mean, Charlie has been just raving about your cooking."

"First of all, he's a friggin liar. I'm a lousy cook, and what's more, I didn't ask you to come back so I could feed you."

The sergeant looked startled. Charlie walked over and kissed her on the cheek.

"Where is Helen?" Jake came out of the back and stopped short when he saw the sergeant. "What's his name, Charlie? Never mind. Your grandfather was Dan McCarthy." It was a statement of fact, not a question on Jake's part.

"I knew I knew him!" Helen exclaimed. "Well, I'll be a son of a bitch. If your hair were white, you'd look just like him. I'll be a son of a bitch."

Now the officer was completely perplexed. He looked to the old-timer Charlie for help, but all he could do was shrug his shoulders.

Jake and Helen told the story of the kindness of old Dan McCarthy showed them many years ago, long before he was born. When they were finished recounting the story, Helen finally remembered their business and led the officers into the kitchen. Seated at the kitchen table was a sad-eyed old man clutching a bottle of beer in one hand and a shot glass in the other. He looked up at the gigantic young sergeant, and he winked.

"Pull up a chair, kid. I want to confess."

He handed the sergeant a gun and poured himself another shot.

CHAPTER 35

A fter sealing the letter, Jake got a slight chill. His mother always said when that happened, someone was walking across your grave. Now that was a happy thought. The briefing was over, and everyone was thoroughly conversant with their individual assignment. This was what it was all about. All the months of training stateside and here over in this secluded section of the English countryside were now finished. At 3:00 a.m., they would march to the mess hall for the traditional breakfast of steak and eggs. Then after that was the routine of, as Jake put it, "saddling up." This is the process where all the paratroopers put on their packs and parachutes, extra ammunition, and extra sidearms. Each man picked for this highly secret assignment was issued a crotch holster, which had a .25 seven-shot automatic with two extra clips. Some of the troopers made obscene remarks about their newly acquired protuberance in the groin area. They related it to their sexual conquests of the not-so-virtuous or so-cold English maidens. But to Jake, the gun was yet another reminder of the role he chose to play. He honestly felt he had a debt to pay for living in the USA. He, at times, likened himself to one of the knights in the Holy War of centuries ago.

This was all done in his own thoughts. He'd never reveal his ramblings to any of the other troopers.

The lieutenant announced, "Detail all present and accounted for, sir."

"Men, it isn't going to be easy. You all know that. Every one of you are volunteers and highly trained. There isn't a reason in this world why we shouldn't all make it home in one piece. The underground has been alerted to watch for us, if we have any need for them. Right next to me is Sergeant Major Robert Riordan of His

Majesty's First Division Fusiliers. He's living proof that the underground can get men off the continent and home safely."

The early morning fog was settling on the men and their equipment as the captain gave what he considered a last-minute pep talk. Jake was hardly listening. His thoughts were of Middie and the girls. It would be afternoon on Fifth Avenue. The kids would be home from school and starting to do their homework. He forced his way back from Fifth Avenue to the fog-filled morning, in England.

"And so, men, I just want to say God bless you all and the drinks are on me when we get back here. Now, before we go, there's someone here who wants to speak to us. Sergeant, bring the men to attention."

Jake gave the command, and as if they were one, the assembled troopers stood straight and motionless. A figure came from a cluster of cars and jeeps. As he came closer, Jake recognized the man. The captain saluted, Jake saluted, and their greeting was returned.

"Morning, Sergeant Ryan, I'm General Eisenhower. My prayers and the country's thanks are with you today. Your men look in good shape."

"They are, sir."

"Good."

Jake was awestruck. The general went to everyone and introduced himself and gave a word of thanks and encouragement to each trooper. *Talk about a moral boost. Eisenhower himself! Damn! The only thing missing now is the national anthem.*

As Eisenhower departed, the troopers filed in two columns toward their plane. Then Jake heard it. "My God, it is. It is!" he said out loud. Every man heard it at the same time, and they straightened even more. "The Star Spangled Banner," was coming over the loudspeakers. What a way to start a mission! This was the way it should be, God and country. Even after they were airborne, their spirits soared, and they all chattered at once. They knew they'd be all right. What could go wrong after that send-off?

CHAPTER 36

The olive-green Chevrolet stopped at the curb, and a tall lean officer stepped into the warm May sunshine.

With two quick strides, he crossed the sidewalk and entered the hallway leading to the Ryan's apartment. Helen's mother was watching from her usual perch at the front window and saw the soldier enter the building. She ran to the stairs and yelled for Helen to come downstairs.

"For Christ's sake, what's the matter, Mom?" Helen was getting very big, carrying the baby. She tried to keep her weight down, but all she seemed to be doing was eating. When she ate, she seemed to feel a little more relaxed. Her doctor was annoyed at her, but as she put it, "Frig him. I'm the one who's carrying this package, not him."

Helen pulled up short at the sight of the Army officer. Her heart sank. She knew the news was bad, and she didn't want to hear it. She didn't want to talk to him.

"Mrs. Ryan?"

"No, I'm her mother. That's her up there."

"Mrs. Ryan, I'm Major General Charles Edwards. May I please come up? I have something to discuss with you." As the general entered the apartment, he quickly glanced around and liked what he saw. There were pictures of beautiful little children on a cupboard and a picture of Sergeant James J. "Jake" Ryan on top of a radio next to an oversize morris chair.

"Sit here, General. Can I fix you some coffee or some tea, maybe?"

"No, thank you, and please sit down."

"Is he dead, General? You can tell me. You've got to tell me. I have to know."

The young general seemed taken aback by Helen's blunt and direct questions. "Mrs. Ryan, didn't you receive a telegram from the secretary of war? What I mean is, that's why I'm here. Usually, we get a reply or at least a phone call in response to our telegrams."

"General, I didn't get any telegram. I don't know why you're here. I haven't heard from my Jake in four months. Here, look at this! Look at this letter. I've been living on this letter since I got it. Now, please tell me why you're here." She fought desperately to control herself. Jake wouldn't want her to break down, and today, Goddammit, she wouldn't!

The general quickly sensed the urgency in Helen's voice and also recognized the fact that the Army had fouled up control along the line. Someone had really blown it this time, and he was the one who had to smooth things over.

"Your husband volunteered for an extremely hazardous mission—behind enemy lines control in France. If I sound vague, please forgive me, but their mission was so top secret that even I don't know all the details about, and I've been cleared for those top-secret reports. Anyway..."

"General, goddammit, is he dead?"

"No, ma'am, he's not."

She sat back heavily in the chair, and tears welled up and started to run from her blue eyes. After a few moments, she composed herself and asked the general to continue.

"Mrs. Ryan, we are positive he's alive, but he is still behind enemy lines. Officially, he's listed as missing in action. But we have strong reason to believe he's in the hands of the underground. We feel that the sergeant's in good hands and will be returned to us as soon as he can be safely transported to England. Now, you'll continue to receive the allotment checks, the same as you've been, and if you care to, you can have the Army doctors at Fort Hamilton take care of you when you're ready to deliver the baby."

The baby, damn! Jake doesn't even know about the baby! I should have told him, but I didn't want to have him worrying about me. Her emotions were mixed as she rationalized her reasons for not writing to Jake about her condition.

CHAPTER 37

As he lay under the tarpaulin, the smell of cow and horse manure made him wretch. He thought he'd pass out. He was wishing he'd pass out. He wondered if he'd suffocate. Boy, would Middie and the girls be proud of him. How did your father die? Well, he suffocated while hiding under a pile of shit. That thought, along with his mental and physical attitude, started him laughing. The laugh was like a child giggling, and he was not able to stop.

The old farmer had the pile constructed in such a way that the side closest to the barn had a plywood square buried under it, going about four feet deep, with another two feet above the ground. He had to grovel through the moist animal leavings, find the tarp and slip into the plywood-covered hole. His wounds pained him, and he wanted to cry out, but the thought of being sent to a concentration camp forced him to be silent.

On many occasions since the Third Reich occupied France, the dung heap had been used to hide British, French, and more recently, American soldiers and pilots. The farmer knew that when the Nazis were looking for an Allied soldier, they would systematically go from farm to farm, searching.

The troops would be very thorough. Their long bayonets would be thrust into the hay piles, and wagons would be overturned as they looked for false bottoms where a man could be hidden. But when it came to the dung heap, only the perimeter would be given a cursory inspection. The bayonets would have to be cleaned if thrust into the heap, and the thought repulsed members of the "master race." Occasionally, an enterprising German soldier would fire a few short bursts into the heap, but because of the density of the compost, the bullets couldn't penetrate to any degree.

Jake had lost count. He couldn't even remember what day it was or when he went into the hole. He didn't know if he had been there for an hour or for a week. He did remember this was the third time he'd been forced into the bowels of the earth. He must have fallen asleep in the vertical coffin. He still didn't know how long he'd been there when three short taps and two long ones on the side of the barn signaled to him that the coast was clear. It was nighttime, and the air was still and warm. The farmer, Le Perche, was seated on a packing crate about ten feet from the dung heap when Jake poked through the tarpaulin. His wounds were really hurting now, and he thought his leg was bleeding again.

CHAPTER 38

Monsieur Le Perche was a tall, slim, silver-haired man in his early seventies. He did not read or write and could not speak English at all except for "Franklin Roosevelt." He had a rotogravure photo of the president folded into a small square tucked into the lining of his weatherworn cap. He'd produce the photo and smile his toothless smile. During WWI, the old man had fought the forces of the kaiser under the command of Marshall Pétain. Now Pétain was collaborating with the Nazis, and from being a hero and semigod, he was despised and hated by every Frenchman who loved his country.

The old man would have stayed neutral except for the day the Germans stopped their convoy alongside the fence that bordered his farm. He didn't realize how much conditions had deteriorated under the figurehead leadership of Pétain. He couldn't believe that in this beautiful country setting, there was violence and instant death to any Frenchman that the troops of the Third Reich deemed expendable.

The ruthlessness of the soldiers hit the old man all at once on the tree-lined road outside his cow pasture. The soldiers had stopped to relieve themselves of their body waste. Even though they were the "super race," they still sat and squatted at the roadside just as any normal man did when the feeling came over him. His grandchildren were in the field, and the sight of fifteen soldiers squatting over a ditch with their rear ends bared and reflecting the spring sunlight was too much of a temptation for them. Maurice and Jacques, nine and ten years old, couldn't resist. They scooped up the hardened cow leavings and started throwing them at the bare-assed soldiers. Their laughter wafted all the way to the barn. The old man came out just in time to see the tall light-haired officer pick up the machine gun and coolly shoot and kill the two babies.

Monsieur Le Perche buried his grandchildren in the family grave-yard out behind his brick farmhouse. He cleared the land with his own hands. His wife, two sons, and now two grandsons were buried on his land. Since the killings, the graveyard had more guests sleeping beneath the fertile soil. Under one headstone were the remains of six Nazi soldiers. Each of them were from the garrison quartered at Le Blanc, a town eight kilometers from the farm. The first one in the forty-foot hole was a six-foot, two-inch light-haired German officer who never came back after a moonlight stroll near the river.

Le Perche had cut off every one of the officer's fingers with a carving knife. He had to revive the "superman" twice. He finally cut off his hands and left him to bleed to death on the floor of the wine cellar beneath the farmhouse. The other five were executed but not tortured by the old man. After the executions, the top layer of dirt was removed from the hole. About a foot and a half down, there were heavy planks that would be removed, revealing the thirty-foot abyss where the enemy soldiers would be unceremoniously dumped.

Le Perche had moved the bodies of his loved ones into one grave. The grave in the center was sacred to the farmer. The one to the left was for the Nazis, and the one to the right was the final rest-ing place for eight Allied soldiers that the underground couldn't save. Every time a German would disappear, the neighboring farms would be searched, but for some reason, the graveyards would be spared. They were so efficient, yet so stupid, the old man thought.

"They are predictable," was what he'd tell the other members of the underground. "That predictability will be their downfall."

Except for the times when he was in the hole, Jake's living quar-ters were in the wine cellar. His nurse was the daughter-in-law of the farmer. She spoke English, but it was heavily accented. She had large brown eyes and long black hair that hung loose around her shoul-ders. Her figure was exquisite, even in the loose-fitting farm clothes she wore. Though pained, he reluctantly responded to the soft and gentle touches of this big-bosomed nurse. When she cleaned his knee wound, she would wash his leg, stopping just short of his maleness. He knew he was getting better because his body was responding to her touch. In the dim light, he hoped she wouldn't notice how he was reacting. He didn't want her to think badly of him. After all, if she got caught by the Nazis, it would be her life. He didn't want to complicate matters by getting aroused and possibly embarrassing or alienating her. It had been so very long since he'd felt a woman. The last time was in Grand Central Station, when he'd kissed Middie goodbye. It seemed like a hundred years ago.

Chapter 39

The dawn was beginning to break as Wally looked out the window. He hadn't missed work in twelve years. As a matter of fact, he couldn't even remember being late. The record was going to end today. He knew it, but he really didn't care. At least he was being helpful. He'd borrowed a car from Tom Healy, the boss of pier six. As for himself, he was sure he'd never need a car, but this was an exception. After all, Middie had to get to the hospital at Fort Hamilton.

She had called him about three thirty and asked him, "Get your friggin ass outa bed and drive me to the fort."

Wally had insisted on being called any hour of the day or night. He didn't want to be deprived of having his moment in the war effort. Besides, he loved Helen with a love that almost equaled the one he had for Jake. Together with the girls, they'd given him more pleasure than he could ever explain. It all started when he and Jake had first met, which was long before either of them knew Middie. Together they were invincible. They would fight, love, drink, and on two occasions, spent the night in jail together. Wally had changed when Jake got married. Jake hadn't, but Wally was so domesticated people would marvel when they found out the social status of the two men.

"Mr. Ryan, you have another daughter."

"I'm not Mr. Ryan. I'm a friend of the—How's Helen? Is the baby okay? You said another daughter?"

Wally was slapping the Army doctor on the back, asking questions and trying to explain who he was all at the same time. Finally, the doctor got the idea and told Wally he or the family would be able to see her in an hour or two. The beaming new uncle left the hospital and headed to the florist at Ovington Avenue and Fifth Avenue.

There he explained to the young Greek couple who owned the shop what he wanted and why. He was ecstatic. Boy, would Jake be happy when he came home! He took the huge bouquet with the baby rattles pinned to the side and headed to the Emerald Bar on Eighty Sixth Street near the movie house.

"Set up the bar. Men, we're going to drink to Jake's newest daughter." Every man at the bar held up their glasses in the sign of toast. "To Jake. May God bring him back to us soon." Wally repeated the toast about twelve times in the next forty-five minutes, and by the time he got to the hospital, he got Helen's "You! You big bum! You're loaded! You're a friggin disgrace. What the hell kind of a proxy father are you gonna be? You're worse than that bastard that got me into this friggin place."

CHAPTER 40

At first, he didn't know where he was when he raised his head. He could hear the rumblings of heavy machinery and the sounds of men shouting and cursing. After about an hour, his nurse, Marie, entered the wine cellar and told Jake that the Germans were being replaced by new troops. She was so excited he could hardly understand her. What the hell was the difference? German soldiers were all the same to him. As long as Le Blanc was occupied, he'd be confined to the dung hole or the wine cellar. Marie took him by his good hand and guided him into the brilliant sunlight. The sky was as blue as Helen's eyes. The old man and his family were waving to the Germans, who were returning their greeting. The old Garrison was completely gone, and the new soldiers were nearly settled. Jake noted it was a panzer outfit. He felt very odd standing there in his peasant clothes, waving to the enemy soldiers.

The last tank had passed when a staff car carrying four high-ranking officers pulled off the dusty road and headed toward the small group of peasants. Jake didn't know what to do. He felt that his heart would leap out of his chest cavity. He was immobile with fear. His mind raced. For a split second, he thought the Frenchies had given him up. But he dismissed it and felt bad for even having the thought.

The highest-ranking officer alighted from the auto, clicked his heels, and gave the Nazi salute. He spoke in the traditional guttural German manner, but he had a refined sounding way of pronouncing the harsh tones of his native tongue. After about a minute or so, the impeccably dressed soldier realized that the peasants didn't understand German. The man smiled and nervously tried his hand at French. It was so bad that Marie held up a hand and asked if he spoke

---

any English. A look of relief came over the man's face as he broke into flawless English, introducing himself and his party.

It was odd, but Jake thought that this Kraut wasn't that bad. He was neat and military, but he had a quality about him, just something. Nothing you could place your finger on, just something. Marie was smiling as she introduced the group to her German commander. When she came to Jake, she introduced him as her brother, who was unable to speak and had trouble understanding—an accident at birth was the way she put it.

The commander nodded as he saw Jake hunched over and staring wild eyes at the soldiers. "Do not be afraid, dumb one. We will not harm you."

"What's this 'dumb one' shit?" Jake almost said out loud, but he didn't.

The Nazi's voice was soothing and concerned. He actually made Jake believe that he was sorry for him. Jake's head twitched involuntarily, and he remembered a movie he'd seen with Middie. It was about a British soldier in India. To avoid being captured, he faked being a mute Svengali native. That was it. That was his cover! A mute Frenchman. The old Garrison commander would have known something was wrong if Jake suddenly appeared. But now the new commandant of Le Blanc would be none the wiser.

He was better now. The weeks passed into months, and the healing process proceeded the way nature had intended. He was able to use his right hand with just the slightest bit of discomfort. His leg wound left him with a slight limp. He exaggerated this when he walked to add to the identity that Marie Le Perche had created for him. The farm food was good. He didn't have much of an appetite anyway, but after working in the fields all day and spying on the movements of the Germans at night, he gained a new respect for food. He actually was enjoying his role-playing as Jacques the mute peasant.

There still wasn't any way he could get away from the Germans. He wanted to reach the mountains and get across the border into Swiss territory and freedom. His wife and girls were constantly on his mind, and when he let himself dwell on it, he became very depressed.

Marie was starting to get to him too. There was the night when he walked down to the river to bathe. He had just stripped to his shorts when she walked into the clearing, naked. The moon shone on her. Her body glistened and shimmered. Her face was brilliant in the pale light. She walked, wordlessly, straight to him and pressed herself against him. She didn't have to, but she told him of her needs and how long she had been widowed, how much she wanted him to make love to her. Jake wanted to resist, but he also wanted her. He tried to control himself, explaining how much he loved Middie. He was weakening. Good god! Anyone would give in! He was a man, and she was a warm, willing, naked, beautiful girl.

His moment of truth was put off when they heard someone calling Marie and walking through the darkness toward them. It was the German commandant. Jake ran to the river, and she headed toward the clump of trees where her clothing was neatly piled. She answered the call and emerged from the tree with her dress hanging loosely on her body. She hastily explained that although her brother, Jacques, was a good swimmer, he did need someone to watch over him because he easily got confused and at times wandered away.

After that night, Jake studiously avoided being alone with her. He knew what his feelings were, and he wanted to be true to Middie. The war wouldn't last forever, and he wanted to return to her with clear a conscience.

CHAPTER 41

It became obvious something was going on. There was almost a constant flow of men and tanks heading into and through Le Blanc. Marie told him of reports that huge underground construction was going on about six kilometers south of the town. The information was sketchy at best, but there was something going on, and by God, Jake was going to find out what it was.

Marie and Monsieur Le Perche rushed into the town hall, very excited. After much shouting between the old man and the guard outside of the commandant's office, the German officer abruptly pulled open the thick mahogany door. His face brightened as he saw Marie in a low-cut peasant dress, standing in the outer office. He quickly silenced the protesting guard and escorted his two visitors into his office, closing the door behind them. She seated herself directly in front of the Nazi major. Fumbling for her handkerchief, she dropped it to the thickly carpeted floor. As she went to retrieve it, she revealed just enough bosom to arouse the keen and complete interest of the man on the other side of the desk. In between sighs and tears, she explained that her brother was missing and that she feared for his safety. She was afraid that one of the soldiers might not realize he was, well, a bit slow and could not hear too well. She would be terribly grateful if he would alert his brave men to be aware that Jacques meant no harm to anyone and was just an "accident at birth." He meant no harm. Again, she dropped her handkerchief and again revealed more than ample amount of cleavage to a mesmerized officer.

When they left his office, he had already called all his patrols and checkpoints, including the area six kilometers to the south of town. He told them not to bother the tall crippled man with the childlike mind. They were to treat him with dignity and care. Whoever found him was to hold him, and the commandant would personally come to collect him and return him to his family. This order included the off-limits areas also. Further, he told the outpost guards that if anyone injured this poor unfortunate, they would answer to him personally. Marie thanked him profusely. Monsieur Le Perche doffed his beret and pumped the man's hand. As they rode back toward the farm in their cart, the old man spat angrily and repeated his view of how predictable the Germans were.

CHAPTER 42

J ake, as Jacques, had seen enough to know that the construction
of an underground complex, completely hidden from the air, was
nearly completed. As best as he could figure out, it would house a full
battalion of tanks, plus the necessary equipment and living facilities
for the crews. All that was visible were air vents protruding about a
foot above the ground. These would virtually be impossible to see in
an aerial photograph of the area. The entrance ramp was in a grove
of large trees and was constructed to hide the sixty-foot-wide cavern
mouth. He took out a piece of charcoal and started to make a draw-
ing on his chest and abdomen. When he finished, he buttoned his
shirt and limped down the hill toward the road leading to the sentry
post. He prayed Marie and the old man had succeeded in getting the
commandant to alert his sentries to his wanderings.

The soldier at the checkpoint saw the tall figure dragging one
foot behind him, heading straight toward his guard post. He called
and connected with the commandant. Jake's heart slowed to its normal pace when he saw the sentry hang up the phone and smile at
the "French peasant" with that "I know you're a nitwit" smile people
always flashed to retarded people. Jake grunted and continued on
down the ramp with the guard trying to pull him back. The soldier
was thoroughly exasperated but didn't want to physically restrain the
unauthorized visitor because he had the sanction of the commandant.

Once inside, he made mental notes of everything. Men were
shouting and obviously cursing at him, but he just wandered about,
occasionally jerking his head and rolling his eyes. He spotted the full
storage area with the air vent directly above the drums of fuel. He
wandered to the living quarters, where he counted bunks for at least

two hundred men. He saw seventy-five new-type tanks. There were huge fans to dispel the carbon monoxide in the garage area.

This place is fantastic! he thought. *How the hell can we destroy it?*

Someone yelled something, and Jake knew from the tone that his Nazi "savior" had arrived to take him "home." He had seen enough. Although he couldn't speak or read German, he spotted the area where the ammunition was stored. The door was painted red and had what was more than likely warning signs posted on the adjacent walls.

The ride home in the roadster almost made Jake laugh. The officer and he sat in the rear of the staff car, and the officer talked all the way to the farm. "I know you can't hear me, but I want you to know that I am your friend. I'm not here to hurt anyone. I don't like the war. I have never killed any innocent ones. I am against the Americans, not the French. The Americans are not a pure race. They are mixed. They brag about it. They mix in from marriages. The "melting pot," they call their country. They're bastards, but not the French."

Jake's mind wandered back to his childhood, and he could hear his mother telling his sisters, "Don't bring home one of those Guineas. Stay with your own kind. Don't mix. Marry an Irish lad." Obviously, the Nazi had never met his mother, yet it seemed odd to him that their ideas both seemed the same. The driver pulled off the main road and headed toward the brick farmhouse. The yard was suddenly alive with people running and shouting. There were eight young men he hadn't seen before. The commandant released the flap on his holster as he leaned forward and said something to his driver. He was a cautious one, this friend of the retarded, this exponent of keeping the German race pure, even though he did want to go to bed with Marie. Yes, he was cautious all right.

The old man ran toward the slowly braking auto, with Marie at his side. She jumped onto the running board and started to shower the German with kisses of thanks. He seemed to relax, and Jake noticed him snap the holster shut. As he got out of the car, everyone was touching him and shaking hands. Marie explained that the men were cousins and friends. They lived on neighboring farms and came to help look for him. All were now around Jacques, shaking his hand

and chastising him at the same time. If he didn't know any better, he would have been convinced that their concern for his safety was genuine family feeling.

CHAPTER 43

It wasn't like the other christening parties. This one was subdued. Oh, all the trappings were there. The barrel of beer on the sideboard of the sink, the platters of cold cuts, the bowls of homemade salads, and the bottles of whiskey lined up for anyone who wanted them. Maisie, Leif, Uncle Lulu, Jimmy, Su-Sue, Jo Anne, Henry, Danny, and Mickey the fireman were all there chattering away, and the neighbors were corning and going at intervals, all greeting one another as they passed.

Helen looked lovely. She wore a pink dress of the latest fashion. She had copied the pattern from *Redbook* magazine and made herself an exact duplicate. Her hair was fixed beautifully, and her blue eyes sparkled. She had gone on a diet and was just a trifle over 110 pounds. She made the dresses and little capes that the girls were wearing and even found time to make the christening outfit for the baby.

Uncle Wally and Joan, Jake's younger sister, were the godparents for little Gloria. Money was tight for Helen, but she was managing fairly well. Wally paid for all the liquor, beer, and meats. The salads were made by Helen, her mother, and Joan. Helen insisted on paying Wally for everything, and she put up such a fuss about it that he took the sixty dollars from her and said no more about it.

When they came back from Our Lady of Perpetual Help on Fifth Avenue, he handed Helen a card. "This is for the baby, Mid. Buy her a little something from her Uncle Wally."

He walked to the kitchen, where all the men had gathered to talk about Jake and the war, as she opened the envelope. Inside were four bills. She pulled them out and saw two one-hundred-dollar bills, a fifty, and a ten.

On the bottom of the card, under the sentiment, he had scrawled, "Don't give me any of your lip. This is for Patty, and that's all there is to that. Love, Uncle Wally."

She looked into the kitchen, caught his eye, and shook her fist at him. He smiled and winked and poured two beers, one for himself and one for their friend Joe Becker, the milkman.

CHAPTER 44

She was just sitting down to write thank-you notes to all their friends and relatives when her mother excitedly ran into the room. "Middie! That general is here again. He just pulled up in front of the house." Middie literally flew to the top of the stairs, half expecting to see Jake with the general.

"Hello, Mrs. Ryan! How are you? And how's the new baby?"

What the hell does he care? "Oh, everyone's just fine, General Edwards. Please come in and have a seat. I hope you have some good news for us."

"Yes, I do. The underground has made radio contact with England. He's alive and well, but still in France. They are just waiting for the first opportunity to get him to either Switzerland or on a sub for England. You know, Mrs. Ryan, that there's always a chance..." She didn't hear, nor care, about anything else the general had to say at that point.

She excused herself from the room and went to their bedroom. Closing the door behind her, she sank to her knees and, in a little child fashion, began to pray. She prayed in the formula prayers the nuns had taught her many years ago. She said the Hail Mary, the Our Father, the Memorare, and the Acts of Faith, Hope, and Charity. She buried her face in the pillow and let herself cry. After what seemed to be an eternity, she composed herself and dried her eyes.

As she went out to the living room, her mother and the general were already seated at the table in the kitchen, having tea. The tailor-made military coat was draped casually over the straight-backed kitchen chair with the hat hung on the upright spindle.

A real regular guy this general is, she thought as she entered the kitchen. "General, I'm sorry, I—"

He held up his hand and smiled a big wide grin. "I understand perfectly. I've been through this before, Mrs. Ryan, and—"

"Please call me Helen."

"All right, Helen. I've been through this before, but I must admit, you're taking this amazingly well for a young woman in your circumstances. I've seen wives actually lose hope."

"That's all I have, General. Hope and faith. I know he'll be home, and I know he's well. He is a tough bastard, and I love him. That love will bring him back to us. I know this. So it's just a matter of time before your underground gets him out. Now, would you like something stronger than tea?"

He liked this young woman. She was pretty, and her home was neat and well-kept. Also, she used all the barracks words without sounding offensive. Yes, Sergeant James J. "Jake" Ryan was a lucky man to have her waiting for him. A real lucky man.

CHAPTER 45

T he plans were made, but he didn't like them.

They were too risky. It could ruin the whole underground setup in that area. He knew that finding the underground garage was important, but so were the lives of the Allied soldiers who would need help in the future. Also, the Germans would kill the entire population of Le Blanc after the attack on the underground complex. What he was looking for was a way to place the blame on the Germans and have an alibi for the townspeople. The commandant wasn't stupid, so a foolproof plan was what was needed to protect the Frenchies.

The underground wanted to just rush into the area and drop explosives down the air shafts, and whoever got away would hide in the hills until it was all over. Jake's theory was to have it appear as if the Germans had fouled up. Thus, reprisals against the town would be unnecessary and not in keeping with German policy. Only when they were overtly threatened or harassed did they take vengeance upon the town that harbored the offenders. The explosive idea was hit and miss. Damage would be done, but in order to kill all the troopers and destroy the complex, they'd have to make sure that the ammunition and fuel areas were completely destroyed.

His argument was going badly. The younger Frenchmen were only looking toward today, he told them. He was looking at the overall picture. The future was also important in ridding their homeland of the invaders.

Abruptly, help came from an unexpected quarter. The old man stood up, and all in the wine cellar fell silent. Marie translated for Jake. The talk was short but firm. "Our American guest is correct. The Germans are predictable. They will slaughter the town and all of us as soon as their place is destroyed. That will not help the other

Americans and English that will need our help in the future. It will not help France if her young men are put to death for a brave but foolish act. Bravery should never be confused with stupidity. France needs its young now and after this war to give us more and more French children. We will find a way to place the destruction firmly on German failure—either man failure or mechanical failure, but certainly German failure."

The old man seated himself on a milking stool, reached behind it, and produced a straw-covered bottle of homemade wine. He placed it to his lips and took a long swallow. He passed it to Jake, who duplicated the old man's action; only he took two long swallows. For an instant, the wine cellar was transformed into Rocco's back room on the Brooklyn waterfront. He blinked himself back to France and passed the jug to the young Frenchman next to him.

CHAPTER 46

The key to the mission was the commandant, and the key to him was Marie. He wanted her, but he was gentleman enough not to take her by force. This in itself was unusual for a German. The tales of how they would and did ravage Frenchwomen had spread all through France. But this commandant didn't permit his troops to violate the local citizenry. Marie would have to play up to this man, win his confidence, do anything. The need was urgent, and the time was short.

She made it a point to bicycle to town every day at the precise time the commandant was leaving his office for lunch. She'd smile, laugh, and be dressed just sexy enough not to be obvious. On four occasions, Jake went with her, making mental notes of guard positions and troop carriers. Just in case something went wrong at the complex, he wanted to be able to take as many Germans with him as he possibly could before they started their reprisals.

Jake had remembered a room between the munitions area and the fuel storage area. It was the only one with a guard in front of it. The red writing on the door had to be some type of warning not to go near or dire consequences would be forthcoming. He had to get back to the complex once more.

Once again, the plans were made. Marie was to accept the open invitation to lunch with the commandant—in his quarters. Jake was to wait until precisely ten minutes after one and then approach the sentries at the mouth of the tunnel. He was to walk, in his retarded fashion, past them and try to find out what was so special behind the guarded door.

Monsieur Le Perche pulled his cart to a halt in front of the commandant's office. He was now known to the guards, and they did not protest too much as he headed toward the outer office. It was exactly six minutes after one. The German threw down his napkin at the sound of the commotion and was heading toward the door when the guard opened it. The farmer started to gesticulate and stutter. Marie questioned him and explained to her host that Jacques had strayed again. Her father was sorry to bother them, but being an old man, he was fearful for his son's safety. The commander was so fair and good to them. He had no other place to turn to.

The one guard raised his rifle as the bushes moved. He took aim at the tall figure coming toward him. His finger tightened on the trigger as the form came into focus. He fired, over his head, but the peasant kept coming closer. The first was a warning shot. This one was going right between the Frenchie's eyes. The other guard knocked the rifle sideways just in time. The slug hit a tree with a thud that almost made Jake slow up. He couldn't follow the shot or even recoil at the sounds. After all, the mute in that movie…what the frig was his name? Harry…Harry Fabersham. In *Four Feathers* or was that the whiskey? Anyway, old Harry Fabersham never let on that he could speak or hear, and he got away with it.

Or did he? Who gives a damn now!

The second sentry was yelling and pointing at the officer, running toward the two soldiers. The old man had conned the Nazi again. He was all right, that old bird, and he was a good drinker too. Jake really laid it on this time. He twitched and grunted and dragged his injured leg. He did his act right into the cavern and right to the door of his concern. He saw the switch box and the heavy brown cable. He saw the writing and later found out it meant high voltage. The lieutenant had obviously gotten orders from his commander. Jake was ushered, gently, into a private office and given a large glass of water. His eyes reached for anything of value to be remembered. He saw the thick brown cable coming through the wall at the crease in the ceiling. All the other cables were black. The one from the guard room was brown. The black ones came from a master box at the front of the cave. The one holding his interest came in from outside the complex. It came from a pole and ran mixed with the phone and telegraph wires that connected the town of Le Blanc with the town of Le Face, some twenty-eight kilometers away.

CHAPTER 47

During the ride to the farm, he watched the wires running overhead from pole to pole. The brown one stopped and ran down the pole and into a clump of bushes. He wasn't really an electronic wizard, but he knew that whatever was in that clump of bushes controlled something very important at the complex.

The next day, Jacques and the old man went early to a small hill about a hundred yards from the clump. At precisely nine o'clock, the staff car, with the commandant himself driving, stopped at the pole. He parted the bushes, and as Jake had focused his binoculars, the German removed a key ring from his pocket, selected one, and opened a large padlock protecting a square concrete box at the foot of the pole. He looked inside, closed the door, snapped the lock, placed the shrubs around it, and returned to his auto. As he negotiated the U-turn, Jake and the old man looked quizzically at each other.

They were relieved by two brothers who stayed on the hill until midnight. Two other nameless French patriots relieved them. Jake returned alone at about eight thirty the following morning. The rain was softly falling, and the grass and earth smelled good. He liked this farm-boy life. He liked the rain. It made the crops grow.

His thoughts went to Brooklyn, and his stomach ached. *What are they doing without me? I hope they're getting along. But if they are, then will they need me when I get back?*

He tried to think of his present problem, but his thoughts kept returning to Middie. He started to picture the girls, and he started crying—not sobbing, just crying.

He dug a watch out of his pocket and marveled at the timing of the German. At precisely 9:00 a.m., the car was pulling to the side of the road. The commandant, again alone, repeated the routine of inspecting the cement box and returning to town. It was a once-a-day inspection at 9:00 a.m. precisely. That was obvious. Again, the old man was right. The Germans were predictable.

CHAPTER 48

It was clear what Marie had to do. Jake didn't like the idea, but it had to be done. Marie sent a note to the commandant, telling him it was important that she meet with him alone at about nine thirty at the farm. Like clockwork, the following day, the roadster pulled to the side of the road. He went directly to the pole, not bothering to look around. He opened the box, looked inside, closed the door, snapped the lock, and rushed to the car.

He was early, but he was also anxious. Marie feigned surprise. "Look at me. I'm not even dressed. I must look a mess." She had a shirt on over her slip. Her blouse was hanging on a tree limb near the large oaken washtub. She was just finishing washing her face. The officer looked at the large smooth, veinless breasts straining against the course woolen slip. It was obvious that she was without any undergarment, as he could see the breasts outlined against the homemade slip. She asked him to give her the blouse, and he did so with a trembling hand.

He followed her into the house with all the anticipation of a young bridegroom. She beckoned him into a chair while she sat opposite him, slowly slipping into her blouse. She explained that her father was ill in bed with a fever and there was no one else around. Her brother was with her cousins in the fields. She asked if it would be at all possible to get one of the doctors from his command to visit her father if he got any worse. The Nazi was sincere. He said he'd be more than happy to send a doctor anytime, day or night.

"Is that all? Is there anything else I can do? Do you need money? Food? Perhaps a pretty dress?" he asked.

Marie stood up and buried her face in her hands and ran upstairs, sobbing. The German found her sitting on a chair outside a room with a large bed. He knelt down and told her he was sorry he had made her cry. She explained that they were tears of joy. He was so nice, and there wasn't anything she wouldn't do for him. His trembling hands reached up and gently pulled her face toward his.

She kissed him warmly and passionately. Sliding off the chair, she fumbled with his tunic and slipped her hand under his shirt, touching his chest. He unbuttoned her blouse while at the same time kissed her swanlike neck. Fully aroused, he kicked off his boots while she unfastened his gun belt and trousers belt.

Suddenly, she stood up and tugged at the military trousers. He stepped out of them, leaving them in the hall. He followed her into the bedroom while she closed the door and locked it. The old man crept up the stairs and silently removed the keys from the German's pocket. He handed them to Louis, one of the farmhands. In the woods, there was a horse tethered. He rode to the hill and gave Jake the keys. Swiftly he raced to the box and, fumbling for the right key, finally got the lock opened. Louis took the keys and rode back to the farm. The old man returned the keys to the pocket and, with tears in his eyes for Marie, returned to his "sickbed."

CHAPTER 49

At eleven thirty, the door opened, and the commandant got dressed and left the house. All was peaceful. He was at ease. He was satisfied. The sun felt good streaming through the windscreen of his auto. He'd been away from his office for too long, but it was worth it. He sped past his 9:00 a.m. checkpoint without even looking. He felt glad to be alive.

At twelve thirty, everyone at the complex would be inside for lunch. Except for four sentries, the 185 men would be in the dining area. In the town, 14 enlisted men would be eating together; 8 officers would dine together, and 2 sentries would be on the street. Monsieur Le Perche had dispatched 15 members of the underground to various positions around the Nazi headquarters. All were heavily armed but had strict orders not to shoot or be seen. It was just insurance.

Le Perche thought of everything. He should have been a general. Jake realized that the box was a self-destruct device that was to be used only if the Germans were being overrun. It was connected to the complex and would destroy it so it could be of no value to the enemy. Realizing he was not electrically gifted, Jake asked Le Perche to find someone who was. The old man had found just such a loyal Frenchman. He spoke enough English to explain to Jake that it was in fact a self-destruct mechanism, battery operated and manually detonated. The idea was simple. If there was a chance of being overrun, the commandant would get to the switch and detonate it, just as Jake had suspected, destroying any equipment that might be useful. The morning check was to ensure that the fail-safe system was still operational and that no one had tampered with it.

Le Perche instructed his man to chop the cable as though an animal had chewed the wires, and then he was, if possible, to short-circuit the mechanisms, thereby detonating it. If, and only as a last resort, the first plan was too complex, he was to manually trip the self-destruct device, and the town would be at the mercy of the troops, as originally anticipated.

The electronics man had already electrocuted a squirrel, which again gave Jake cause to marvel at the intelligence of the peasants. Once the blast destroyed the complex, the commandant would go to the box, find the open lock, the "chewed-through" cables, and the electrocuted squirrel. They were banking on the fact that the German was a fair man and would blame himself for not locking up the box in his haste to get to Marie and he would accept the punishment for failure, which was certain to be death. The plan proceeded without a flaw. The simplicity of it was what made it so workable.

The explosion rocked the countryside for miles around. Windows in the town were blown out. All thought the invasion had begun. The mayor ordered the air-raid sirens to be sounded, and confusion prevailed. The commandant and two officers checked the complex.

Unable to get through, they drove to the box. Without waiting for the car to stop, the frenzied commandant leaped to the roadside. Stumbling and crawling, he made his way to the cement bunker and saw exactly what the old Frenchman wanted him to see. Jake didn't understand German, but he knew that Herr General Henrie Von Siebenheller was blaming himself for the accident.

That evening, the roads were alive with ambulances, wreckers, and men all moving into the complex area. The patrols that normally kept watch along the beach areas were pulled out to assist in rescue operations.

Jake was taken to the beach, where a waiting motor launch would take him out to sea. He was glad that Marie hadn't come to see him off. She had not come out of her room since that morning. He went to her door, but the low sobbing sounds coming from within made him feel uneasy. He wanted to thank her. He felt she had done it partly for him. He scrawled some lines on a piece of paper and slipped it under the door.

As the cool sea mist assaulted his face, a strange sadness possessed his mind and body. The faces of the old man, Marie, Louis, Andre, even Von Siebenheller would remain etched in his inner thoughts for years to come. He knew he'd miss them and was saddened by the knowledge.

CHAPTER 50

Jake said, "Hello, Joe, only three more weeks to go." The big man with the oversize hands smiled and waved to Jake.

"How come you're so nice to him, Jake? You never have a snide remark or under-the-breath insult to Mr. Becker," I asked.

"That big palooka is one of the grandest men I've ever known. He'd do anything for you or me or anyone. He's been a milkman for almost forty years, but he's been a real friend of mine for over thirty. During the war when I was away, he'd see to it that Middie was all right and the kids always had plenty of milk. When it was raining or snowing, he'd give a ride to the girls to school in his horse wagon just so they wouldn't get wet."

"Jake, you're an old softy. Little things mean a lot to you. I'd never have believed that under the checkered shirt there's really a heart."

He gave me one of those looks that would let you know just what he was thinking. He didn't curse much, but he could call you names with his eyes. I smiled, finished my coffee, and left as he started to berate Sammy Plotkin, the retired tailor. As the door closed, I could hear him telling Sam not to cross the imaginary line Jake had drawn.

"No Jews on this side of the line unless you got money. You got any money?"

"Don't pay any attention to him, Sam. You can come over and sit by me anytime."

"Helen, you're too nice to be married to…to…to him."

Sam wanted to curse, but he didn't out of respect for Helen. Daily, the ritual was followed. Sam would come in to buy two containers of coffee for Joe, the barber, as well as his father. Jake would tease Sam and forbid him to sit near Helen. Sam would protest.

Helen would protect him, and Jake would continue to berate the "old Jew bastard."

One morning, Jake hadn't come out of the back yet, and Sam had come to buy the coffee. He looked around, and the disappointment was evident across his face. "Where's Jake? Is he all right?" he asked, almost gasping the words. "He's not sick or anything, is he, Helen?"

"No, he's inside, getting dressed. He'll be out in a few minutes."

Sam smiled and sat down on the leather-covered swivel stool. "Good. Then I'll wait for him to give me Joe and Pop's coffee."

"Ya know, Sam, you're a loony bastard. If I had someone talk to me the way he talks to you, I'd never come in here at all."

"I like Jake. I know he's only fooling. He's interested in me, and he makes me laugh. He likes to tease me. You see, Helen, I have nobody. I am an old man, and I'm alone. I look forward to seeing him. If it wasn't for you and him, I'd never have anything to smile about. I hope you understand."

He stopped and looked at Helen, and she could sense the loneliness of the old man. He added pleadingly, "But please don't tell him that I'm not offended. It might spoil it for him." She looked at him and felt sorry. She was glad that she had Jake and the girls. "I won't tell him, Sam. I won't."

CHAPTER 51

U pon his return to England, he was sent to a hospital just outside of Surrey. The countryside was beautiful. There were woods filled with wild game and birds of every description. Each morning, at about four thirty, he'd slip into his robe and open the doors leading to the veranda area. There he'd sit and drink in the sounds of nature, with the tip of his cigarette casting an eerie reddish glow on his face, illuminating his gaunt features.

His thoughts were sober. They'd alternate between France and Brooklyn, Brooklyn and France. He was unable to get any news about the Le Perche family, but he rationalized that maybe it was just as well. He wanted to think and believe they were fine. He blotted out the thoughts of German reprisals and turned his mind to Helen and *home*.

There was quite a backlog of mail for him to read and reread. There hadn't been enough time since he had gotten back for new letters to reach him. He had to satisfy himself with letters written before he went on his mission; the news was a bit ancient. He was told on his return that Helen and the family were fine. He'd seen the confirmation that the cablegram to her had been received and acknowledged.

He was getting impatient to leave England and return to Brooklyn. His patriotic hunger had been satiated. He had been honored by his country and by the government, in exile of France. Although the citation for his Silver Star didn't go into the details of the original mission, it had spelled out the personal peril Sergeant First Class James J. Ryan had endured. The Distinguished Service Cross, the Silver Star, the Bronze Star with the *V* for *valor*, the Army Commendation Medal, the Purple Heart, and the Combat Infantry

Badge were all worn in their proper position on the left side of his uniform. Along with his new stripes, the French Cross of Gallantry and the Croix d' Guerre were worn with pride tinged with sadness— sadness that, had he dwelled on it, might have put a pall over his homecoming.

The leg wound wasn't painful anymore. He knew he'd have a permanent limp, but that didn't really bother him as much as the partial loss of hearing he'd be forced to endure the rest of his life. He hadn't lost all the hearing in the ear, but it was just enough for him to have to strain to hear when people spoke to him while standing to his left.

The trip home on the troopship, *General Patch*, was long and boring for him. He wanted to fly, but the Army doctors felt that a long sea trip would be beneficial to his recuperation. His status as a wounded hero and a first sergeant did entitle him to special treatment, but he didn't avail himself of any of these privileges. His refusal to discuss how he had received his decorations added an aura of mystery to the quiet man seen walking the decks, always alone, and wrapped in deep thought.

CHAPTER 52

"Mr. Ryan, a man your age should know better than to go jumping out of windows."

"I told him that, Doc, but he's as loony as they come. I told him to let the firemen do their job, but no, he had to go play friggin Errol Flynn!"

"Middie, please leave me alone. I hurt all over."

This was the first time in almost thirty years that Jake had gone for a physical examination. The only time since his Army days that he'd been to a doctor was when he had the accident on the pier. The reason he was there today was very simple: he hurt from his head to his shins.

A week ago, he was in his kitchen at about five in the morning. As usual, he couldn't sleep. So he went to the icebox for a can of beer. He'd just opened it and was lighting a cigarette when he saw a flash and heard a small popping sound. He looked hard into the morning darkness and realized that the house behind him was on fire. Calling for Helen, he pulled on a pair of trousers that were in the laundry basket.

"Call the fire department! George De Angelis's house is on fire!"

"Jake, where the frig are you going?"

"Out the window. It's the quickest way."

"Bullshit! That's an eight-foot drop to the ground. You'll—"

"Aw, shut up and call." He opened the window to the courtyard and jumped.

He hit the ground and stumbled, scraping both knees and ripping his trousers. Once on his feet, he climbed, with difficulty, the fence separating the De Angelis house from Jake's alleyway and started banging on the side door.

Finally, he took the milk box and broke the storm door window and inside window. He turned the handle, reached in between the jagged window fragments, and let himself into the house. Groping and gagging, he began yelling and banging on the walls. There were flames in the kitchen near the stove.

The flame wasn't that furious, but the heat and smoke were unbearable. He could hear people coming from upstairs, but he couldn't see them. He called, and he heard George answer. He was able to find the front door, and the blast of air momentarily felt good. George took out the two youngest. His wife, Janet, had little Janet in her arms, and Jake helped George's mother to the safety of the sidewalk.

The engines pulled to a halt, and about a dozen men, clad in rubber, sprang to action. Understandably, George was concerned for his family and his house. So Jake just wandered off around the corner to finish his beer and have a cigarette, not wanting any thanks.

As he sat at the table in his shorts, Helen was cleaning the scrapes with peroxide and asking him a dozen questions at once. He just nodded and grunted until she was exasperated.

"Ya big son of a bitch, answer me!"

He took her in his arms, held her close, and said, "Come on, Mid, let's go to bed."

"Who can sleep with all that racket that the firemen are making?"

He pinched her behind and asked, "Who said anything about sleep?"

She playfully swatted his arm and led her hero to their bedroom, not trying very hard to conceal her pride in her man.

"You take these, Mr. Ryan, and rest in bed. When you jumped out the window, you pulled your chest muscles, and you swallowed enough smoke to last you a lifetime. But your heart is good, and your pressure is normal, so I'm sure you'll survive. Make sure he gets some rest, Helen. No exercise of any kind."

"I'm glad you said that, Doc. He's become a regular sex maniac. Maybe this will calm him down." She winked, and the doctor smiled.

CHAPTER 53

There were parties and even a parade. It started at OLPH Church and went to Sunset Park, where taps were blown, and he was forced to lay a wreath at the base of the flagpole. Looking at the pole, he felt stupid. It was badly in need of paint, the flag was faded, and there was the unmistakable smell of urine rising from the surrounding cement. Undoubtedly, Uncle Lulu and his contemporaries had left their water there after finishing their jug of muscatel.

He was getting tired of the fuss that had been made about his return. Actually, it was the drinking that was getting to him. Everyone wanted to buy him a drink and bask in the reflected glory of being a personal friend of the neighborhood hero. He would have put a stop to the ceremonies as soon as they started, but a lot of people put much effort into them, and he didn't want to disappoint them. Also, Middie seemed to be enjoying the goings-on. So if it made her happy, he'd go through with it.

It wasn't the least bit hard for him to adjust to the new addition in his household. One night, after a "welcome home" party at the Carpenter's Hall on Sixth Avenue, he was getting ready for bed. He walked into the baby's room and stood staring down at the fat-cheeked little pink bundle and just couldn't fight back the tears. He was so glad to be home, and he was proud of Helen and the way she handled the dual role he'd forced upon her. She came into the room and just stood by his side.

Finally, she punched him in the rear end. "Let's get to bed, ya big bastard, or I'll hit ya with a pot or something."

The flurry of neighborhood appreciation and recognition came to an end when Jake finally took off the Army brown for the blue denim of the dockworker. His job was waiting for him—which, for the returning vet, was the exception rather than the rule—when the war finally ended. Because of his wounds, he was discharged earlier than he should have been, so there wasn't the rush of returning men looking for their jobs.

CHAPTER 54

Early one evening, Wally came to Jake, his face flushed red and his eyes wide with anger. Jake had never seen his friend this angry. The muscular arms were bulging beneath the work shirt, and the veins in his neck were pulsing with a deep-purplish-blue hue. Placing his hand on his friend's forearm, he momentarily thought he'd grabbed the limb of a tree.

"Hey, what's the matter, Big Nose?"

"Jake, you're not gonna believe this, but—"

"Calm down, Wally. Take it easy and tell me."

His voice trailed off as he saw the unmistakable stain on his right shoulder. "Good god, Wally! You're bleeding. What the—"

"Those dirty bastards started saying wrong things about your Middie and me about when you were away. I was in McCarthy's, and I overheard them. The rotten bastards were laughing. They didn't know I was standing there at the bar. I told them to shut up, and it started. Jake, you wouldn't believe what they were saying—that the baby wasn't yours! They said she's mine." Grabbing him by the arms and in a plaintive tone, he looked Jake in the eyes. "Jake, for God's sake, you know it's not so. I swear to you that—"

Jake interrupted Wally by embracing him as only two friends could. "I'm not even going to give you an answer, Big Nose. I just want you to know that I think you're the finest man I've ever known and anyone who could think things like that has to be lower than…" He didn't finish. He didn't have to.

Wally straightened and just said, "Thanks."

On their way to Lutheran Hospital, Wally was returning to normal. He was describing what had transpired and what the back room of McCarthy's looked like. He really hoped that the damage wasn't too extensive, but if it was, he'd pay for it.

"Ya know ya can't trust a Guinea, Jake. I never felt anything one way or the other about them, but that bum that got me with the knife really annoyed me. He didn't have to do that. He coulda have fought like a man."

Smiling, Jake replied, "Yeah, you're right, Big Nose. You're right."

CHAPTER 55

Just recently I was in the store for my usual morning cup of coffee and my catchup on all the neighborhood news. Helen came out of the back, laughing out loud, with tears running down her plump freckled face. Jake just turned, looked at her, and mumbled something about her being "off her rocker." I started laughing at her laughing. She couldn't stop, and I couldn't either. Jake thrust a piece of paper into my hand, and I finally gained composure to read it. It was a legal document notarized and stamped. It was Helen's last will and testament, which went as follows:

> I, Helen Margaret Ryan, being of sound mind and body, do hereby declare in the event of my death, I leave all my worldly possessions to my husband, James J. Ryan, to do with as he wishes, unless he decides to marry or obtain a girlfriend, in which case all said goods and monies go to my favorite charity, which is the Canadian Club Liquor Company.
>
> To my daughter Kathleen, I leave the responsibility of praying me into heaven.
>
> To my daughter Erin, I leave her her husband, Daniel, and her mother-in-law.
>
> To my daughter Tara, I leave her her beer and roommates (which I think are all males, but I can't prove it).
>
> To my lovely daughter Gloria, I leave her beauty, charm, and my apartment.

To my good friend Frieda, I leave my mop,
garbage pails, and a can of Ban deodorant.
To my good friends Joseph and Margaret
Becker, I leave my milk order.
To all the rest, I leave nothing.
PS: To Renken's Milk Company, I leave all
my size 42D bras to use as warmers for the cows.

When she calmed down enough to become intelligible, she told me she'd just received her copy of the will from her lawyer, Jake D'Ambrosia. One afternoon, she and Pat were watching one of those "goddamn soap operas" when the heroine decided to make out her will. So Pat got the bright idea to make one for her mother. Thus, the "lovely daughter" accolade made reference to herself. Helen signed it and mailed it out to Jimmy, the lawyer. He came to the store and notarized and sealed it and asked permission to xerox it and pass it around to his colleagues to brighten their day. Helen agreed, and when Jimmy left, he, like practically everyone else who left their company, was smiling just because of having been in the Candy Store.

CHAPTER 56

I came into the store one afternoon in the early spring. The sun was bright, and the air was clean and clear. It was the time of year when everyone seemed happy, but inside it was a completely different atmosphere. Helen was at the end of the counter in her chair. Jake was seated next to her. Pat was behind the counter, with her children quietly seated at the stools.

With the exception of Jake and Joe Becker, who was at the candy counter, it was obvious that they'd all been crying. I knew I'd come into a real family crisis, and I started to leave, but Jake called me to wait. We'd been friends for quite a while, and he felt he owed me an explanation of the prevailing mood.

I was aware that Pat's husband, George Phelan, was listed as a prisoner of war in North Vietnam. They'd gotten word through the Red Cross that he was wounded but was responding to treatment. They all wrote to him once a week and enclosed their messages in one envelope This circumvented the Vietcong rule about no more than one letter a week. Periodically, a letter would arrive, either typed or written, in someone else's handwriting. Its language was definitely not that of George's, and the message was more propaganda than the words of a man who'd been away from home for nearly four years.

The Red Cross had informed them that he was unable to write due to injuries to his hands, so an English-speaking nurse would take down his words as he spoke them to his family. They were sorry that they were visually unable to verify that George was, in fact, alive, but the Vietcong swore that he was in a maximum-security camp north of Hanoi. The reason he was being interned at the camp was because he was considered to be plotting against his captors to gain his freedom so that he could return to fight against them. (Jake was proud of that part.)

George and Pat were childhood sweethearts. They went to OLPH Grammar School together and were constant companions through high school. George had won a Naval Reserve Scholarship to the College of the Holy Cross in Worcester, Massachusetts, and Helen and Jake had to nurse their lovesick little girl through the "agony of being separated from George." Jake felt she was being a bit dramatic, Helen thought she had a "friggin screw loose," and her sisters knew exactly how she felt. The truth of the matter was, in actuality, she was a bit dramatic but did truly miss him and was thoroughly in love with him.

Pat had secured a job on Wall Street, and what with holidays and vacation time, plus a few scattered dance weekends, she and George weren't the parted lovers that she feared they'd be. The four years flew for others but dragged for the couple. Kathleen had entered the convent and was teaching at a Dominican school in Alexandria, Virginia. Erin had gotten married to a fireman, and they were expecting their third child. Tara, the prettiest of the girls, was an airline stewardess. Of all the girls, she most resembled Helen when she was a young woman.

Upon graduation, George elected to take a commission in the Marine Corps as a second lieutenant. Their wedding was a military one at Our Lady of Perpetual Help. The day was lovely, and Pat was radiant. Helen cried. Jake felt foolish in his tuxedo, but together, he and Helen made a splendid-looking couple.

That was eight years ago. George was a major now, being promoted while in captivity. Pat and he had three children: George, Janet, and Timmy. After the news of his capture, Pat had moved in with her parents. She had been getting phone calls from "some goddamn hippies," as Helen said, telling her they were glad to learn of his capture because he was in an immoral war. Jake and Helen wanted her with them to help her over the initial impact of his captivity. Helen knew just how she felt, for twenty-five years ago, she'd been through the same thing.

Pat knew that George wasn't writing or dictating the letters that she'd been receiving. They were laced with anti-American sentiment, and the personal parts were not what George said or thought. She kept telling herself that the Vietcong would not continue to send letters if George was dead. No one could be that low. The Navy Department was extremely solicitous to her, and the financial aid was enough for her to make ends meet. The separation would have been unbearable if not for the children, Helen, Jake, and the people of the Candy Store.

CHAPTER 57

Her children knew him only from the photographs that were in the apartment behind the store. She was convinced that she had no tears left to shed, but today proved how wrong she was. The Navy Department had just sent a Marine Corps colonel to tell her that George has been killed by the Vietcong three months after his capture. He had been wounded when the villages he and his company were protecting were overrun. After his wounds had healed, he organized the other prisoners to escape. The VC had an informer who gave them the plan. So they took George out and executed him in front of the other prisoners. This had been revealed to them by a Marine sergeant who had recently escaped and made it to an American outpost.

The colonel further told them that the sergeant, a man named Peter Fox, had told them he'd killed the informer shortly after George was executed. Pat thanked the colonel and just sat there, stunned and bewildered. How inhumane, how utterly inhumane, to murder a man for doing what he had sworn to do if captured and to give such false hope to his family for all those years. The effect was numbing.

As I left Jake, I was looking at the ground with my heart feeling as low as the pavement. What a waste of a fine young American man! What a total blow to the freckled-faced young girl. What was going to happen to her children? As the day progressed for me, I couldn't stop thinking of the news. Suddenly, it was as if a light went on in my brain. I still felt terrible for Pat and the children, but I was very proud of George. It wasn't a waste of an American man. It was a contribution to ensure that his children and their children would be free to choose their own direction and way of life and not have to fear the government. I was proud to have known George and proud of what he and thousands of others had done and would continue to do any time freedom was threatened and our country was asked to help.

CHAPTER 58

"Well, well, don't you look nice in your brand-new suit. My, my, you are the handsome devil."

"Thank you, Helen. I know you and Charlie Bennett conspired together to help me. And arresting that old man was just the push I needed to get back into the detective division."

"I was kind of hoping there was something I could do for you and your family. I'm not really good at this, but if there's anything at all I can do to show my appreciation, I'd be very happy."

She interrupted him and tried to make light of what she'd done. But all the time she was trying to figure out how to ask him if he was married or not. He'd be perfect for her Pat. Now, how could she arrange this?

The door opened, and Pat and the kids came bouncing in, all talking and trying to tell their grandmother everything all at once. The young detective sergeant looked at Pat and obviously liked what he saw. Helen saw his glance go to Pat's hand, where her wedding ring was, and once he saw the gold ring, he busied himself in finishing his coffee.

"Dan, I'd like you to meet my daughter Pat and her kids." As he got up from the stool, Helen quickly added, "Her husband was killed in Vietnam. We found out about a year ago." Pat gave her mother a glance but otherwise didn't show her annoyance at the remark. Since the initial shock had passed, her mother kept trying to match Pat with everyone she could.

He stood and greeted her warmly and expressed his sympathy for her misfortune. Pat explained the circumstances and the fact that he'd really been dead for nearly five years. The small talk continued, and Helen's mind was whirling. She seized the opportunity when Dan asked the ages of the children.

Helen interrupted and asked, "Do you have any children, Dan?"

"I better not, Helen. The department frowns on bachelors with children."

Pat smiled, and Helen sighed. Now, to figure out how to get him interested in her and the three kids. What a catch he'd be for Pat! After all, George was dead, and Pat hadn't so much as even looked at another man during all the time they thought he was in captivity. She and the kids were entitled to the protection and love that a good man could give. And Helen could tell he was a good man. His face was kind. He probably took after his grandfather.

CHAPTER 59

It had been raining for nearly a week straight. The piers were busy and behind schedule. This was the third time that Jake could remember the waterfront was this busy. First was for the "Big War," as he put it; then Korea; and now the late sixties, 1969 to be precise. The buildup in Southeast Asia demanded that the men produce, but the weather was slowing them down. They became extracautious because of the slickness of the decks.

Wally called Jake into his office. As he came to the door, his mind flashed, as usual, to twenty-six years ago with Dooley and the others.

"What's the matter today, Big Nose?"

"Ya know, Jake, we're so behind schedule that we're lonesome."

"We gotta get some speed out there."

"I know, but the damn rain has everyone sliding and flopping all over the place. That new guy we got, Abe Hurtado, just fell and broke his arm."

"Jake, I know, but we've gotta get these ships loaded and outa here. The captains are all moaning, the coast guard is moaning, and most of all, the owners are starting to grumble. See if you can get those guys to do a little extra."

"All right, Big Nose, I'll save your job for you. But I don't know why, 'cause I don't even like you."

"Maybe if you cut down their beer breaks, you'd get something done out there for a change."

"Yousa, Mista Boss Man. Yousa Massa Wally." With that, he shuffled out of the office.

He gathered his men around him and told them of the dilemma that Wally was facing. The improvement was noticeable, and before lunch, the men agreed to take only fifteen minutes and then continue to work right through till quitting time. This was clearly against the union rules, but the rules could be circumvented if all the men agreed.

Most of them, at one time or another, had asked for and received a favor or two from either Jake or Wally. So this was their way of saying thanks to the two men.

CHAPTER 60

The noise was deafening. The pallet hit the deck and split the air much the same as the rear of a cannon. A crate of helicopter replacement parts slid along the wet metal directly toward Denny Quirk. Jake was standing on the hatch cover to hold number 3. At the sound, he yelled and yelled to Quirk. Instinctively, he jumped and pushed the longshoreman to safety. The hurtling missile caught him full force on his left side. It wasn't until four days later, when he fully regained consciousness, that he found out what had happened to him after the boom hoist cable snapped. Wally told him that after he was hit by the crate, he was thrown into the number 2 hold. Besides all the assorted broken bones, he had a fracture at the right side of his skull.

The recovery process was slow and boring for Jake and also unbearable for Middie. The union benefits covered the medical bills, but in the beginning, Helen could have cared less about bills. All she wanted was for her Jake to recover. But now, having him around the house all day was beginning to wear her patience thin. She finally had about all of him that she could take. So one day she called the doctor.

"Hello, Doc, this is Helen Ryan. You gotta help me out, Doc. This big bastard is driving me crazy. Everything I do he checks on. If I cook, he's in the friggin kitchen. If I sew, he's in the parlor. The only place I can go by myself is to the john, and I think he'd come in there if I left the door open. Doc, tell him he can go out. I'd even like to see him drinking beer—anything just to get him back to normal again."

"All right, Helen, put him on the phone, and I'll talk to him."

The doctor's words were music to Jake. He hummed for the first time in eight weeks, showered, and shaved. He looked at his body. The irregular lines where the doctors at Lutheran Medical

Center had sutured his open skin together were purple and red. They didn't hurt, but they sure were ugly looking. He really wanted to get out. Being cooped up with Helen was driving him crazy. She's either in the kitchen cooking or in the parlor sewing, and lately, she was spending more time in that goddamn bathroom. She never had time to sit and just talk.

As he came into the kitchen, Helen had a plate of sandwiches and a large glass of milk on the table. Without speaking, he sat and ate three monstrous ham-and-swiss-cheese sandwiches. With two swallows, he reduced the full glass to a container with white droplets left clinging to its sides. Wiping his mouth with a napkin, he reached over and patted Helen on the rear end. He was happy knowing she was giving him the "green light" to go out and get drunk.

She felt a bit apprehensive but was satisfied that at least he had something in his stomach to soak up the beer. He was only going to the corner, but she knew he wasn't fully recovered. She was just glad he was alive and able to go for a few beers. Her mind went back to the day she saw the dent in the potato pot when Jake was missing. She remembered her feeling then and was happy to have him safe and alive.

CHAPTER 61

"Well, hello! This is a very pleasant surprise. How are those fine children of yours?" Pat stepped back and, for a brief moment, couldn't place the smiling young man standing before her. Finally, she spoke when his face registered with her memory bank.

"Sergeant McCarthy, how are you? At first, I didn't…I mean, I forgot…"

"I know what you mean. I have the kind of face people like to forget."

"That's not true, Sergeant—"

"Please, call me Dan, if you don't mind."

"What I meant, Dan, was that you have a very nice face and anyone who would want to forget it would be foolish." She blushed when she realized what she had said, and he caught the pink flush on her freckled face.

"Thank you, Pat. That's nice of you to say."

Knowing she was embarrassed, he quickly switched the subject to inconsequential small talk about her mother and father, the store, Charlie Bennett, and the weather. Then both ran out of things to say and stood awkwardly looking at each other. Pat thought he was magnificent looking, and he thought she was beautiful.

"Well, I must be leaving, Dan. It was nice seeing you again. Please stop at the store when you have a chance. I know my parents will be happy to see you."

"I'd like that myself, Pat. Listen, I have two tickets to the hockey game at the Garden next Thursday. I was wondering, well, I know it's unusual, but you'd…well, would you like to come with me? I'd have you home early, and I'd really enjoy the company."

"It's funny, Dan, but I like hockey. My husband and…" Her voice trailed off.

"I am sorry, Pat. I didn't mean to bring up any memories."

"Really, Dan, I'm the one who should be sorry. I'll never forget him, but he is gone and… Well, I hope you understand because I can't explain it. It's not as if it happened just now. He's been gone for years, actually. And yes, I'd love to go to the hockey game. They're playing the Bruins, I believe?"

Later that evening, when Pat was home, she said to Helen, "Mother, I met Dan McCarthy at A&S today, and he asked me if I'd go to the hockey game with him. I told him I would."

CHAPTER 62

Helen beamed. She was ecstatic. This was just what the doctor ordered. Ever since they found out for certain what happened to George, something had been missing from Pat. Helen could never put her finger on it, but there was something different. When she discussed the subject with Jake, he usually gave her a look or grunt, but he never really commented.

It wasn't the way she talked or looked. She was just a little less bubbly or enthusiastic than in other years. Even when they thought he was in captivity, everything she did, from housework to waiting on the customers, was approached with zeal.

Now, when she spoke of Dan, the girlishness came back. Helen was satisfied that her daughter was getting over the six-year heartache.

The game went into overtime, and they were a little later than Dan thought they'd be. He had made a reservation for two at Gallagher's Steak House near the Garden. He was willing to cancel and drive her directly to Brooklyn. He didn't want to, but he knew that her mother had to open the store early and she had to get her children ready for school. He wished it was Friday night.

"Pat, I know it is a little bit late, so if you want, I'll cancel out the reservation and take you home. I don't have to be at work until six tomorrow night, but I know that you have an early day."

"Well, that's very thoughtful of you, Mr. McCarthy, but are you sure you're not just trying to starve a poor girl to death?" He was relieved and pleased with her sense of humor. Yes, she was a special person, this pretty girl who was walking beside him. He was glad he asked her to go out with him.

CHAPTER 63

After many consultations and much pushing and poking by various surgeons, specialists, and "anyone else who was in the vicinity," Jake was told that his days on the waterfront were coming to a close. He fought and grumbled, but the insurance company that covered the union employees refused to cover him any longer. His spine was in such a state that a fall could possibly result in paralysis. Even with a timekeeper's job, he'd occasionally have to go onto the piers and ships. The company wasn't willing to risk carrying him with a full pay any longer. The union would have to derive some means of compensation amenable to both themselves and the company.

His lawsuit against the company was automatic. It was termed a "no hard feelings" suit. The fact that the accident was an injury that was a direct result of defective equipment made Jake's case a strong one. The insurance company and the steamship line employed were both reputable and knew that if they went to court, they'd surely lose, and the settlement would be a sum of money far more than Jake was asking.

He was a fair man and never believed in getting something for nothing. Middie, on the other hand, was cajoling, nagging, threatening, and pleading with Jake to go to court with his case. Th family lawyer, Jake D'Ambrosio, agreed with Jake. He knew him well and knew that he had deep convictions that would make a court fight for money very distasteful to Jake. On the other hand, Helen had a point. Financial security for both of them and their children and grandchildren loomed within easy reach. A little "acting" on Jake's part as a settlement of three quarters of a million was not beyond the realm of possibility.

Jake's decision was made, and with Jimmy, the lawyer, at his side, he went to the company's insurance carrier and told them that he was willing to settle out of court. The company was prepared for almost anything but this. The adjuster was taken aback and immediately phoned the main office in Hartford. The powers that be suspected some type of chicanery. Apparently, they weren't used to dealing with honest men. After an hour and a half had elapsed, Jimmy finally asserted himself. In his best legal tone of voice, he declared that if his client was subjected to any further delay, they would be forced to reconsider their offer and contemplate a jury trial.

Jake was patient, but even he was growing tired of the delay. After one further phone call to Hartford, the adjuster, Frank Gaffney, presented Jake with a cashier's check for "Holy damn, $220,000!" payable to James J. Ryan. He must have signed eighteen pages of releases, each one perused and approved by his friend and attorney.

After about a month of doing nothing at all except drinking beer, Jake decided to try his hand at running a business. This would be his first endeavor into the world of high finance. Talking with Wally over a beer in the back booth of McCarthy's old place, they decided he was best suited to be the owner of a (you guessed it) bar. The Emerald on Eighty-Sixth Street was for sale and reasonably priced. In their minds, they fantasized what it would be like. By 1974, Wally would retire, and he might even become partners with Jake. It would be great. Of course, they would both take an oath not to drink while working...

Yeah, right.

CHAPTER 64

"Have you gone out of your friggin mind? You'll have more than back problems if I hear you mention buying a bar again. You're bad enough just passing one, let alone owning one. First of all, you'd be drunk every day. Second, you'd have every freeloading son of a bitch in Bay Ridge lined up for free drinks and a handout. I'd wind up in the street on home relief, and you'd wonder where the money went. Jake, I'm warning you, if you mention bar again, find yourself a new place to sleep."

> Under new management
> Grand opening
> December 4, 1969
> Helen and Jake Ryan
> Proprietors

"Now I ask you, Jake, where could you get a better deal than this? We have our own business and an apartment in the back. It'll be tough getting organized for a while, but I'm sure we'll manage. Once we get a routine set up, we'll be able to make things easy for ourselves. You'll see, Jake. You know I'm right. If you had the Emerald Bar, you'd wind up like Uncle Lulu. And we don't need another one in the family."

He agreed, but he also disagreed. He knew she was right, but... well, it would have been nice to see if he could make a go of a saloon. And what with Wally talking about retiring in a few years, it would have been great. But who could argue with Helen, especially when she was right?

CHAPTER 65

On Mondays, the Candy Store was closed, and Jake usually went to New York City to browse around the shops and to buy clothing for the grandchildren. He loved the hustle and bustle of Delancey Street. The Jew boys would do their best to sell at the price listed on the tags, and he'd do his best to get them to sell to him at a lower price. It wasn't that he was cheap. It was just that he enjoyed the arguments with the shop owners. He learned a lot from Sam at the Candy Store, and he employed Sam's techniques on Delancey Street. He'd walk from Delancey to the Bowery, along the Bowery to Canal Street, and then over to Broadway. Once at Broadway, he'd turn south and head over to Joe Maxwell's on Reade Street and Broadway. There he'd avail himself to the free lunch and quaff a number of tall cool Schaeffers before taking the Fourth Avenue subway at city hall to Bay Ridge.

His spirits were high when he pushed open the iron folding gate that protected the front of the store. He called for Helen, Pat, and the kids. No one answered. So he went to his icebox and took a beer. He drank it down without stopping. He had put his parcels on the marble countertop. He opened another beer and wondered aloud as to everyone's whereabouts. The knocking on the front window silenced him. He peered through the front window and saw Frieda, the woman Jake referred to as Garbage Gertie.

In her early seventies, she had developed a fetish for stacking garbage in the street litter baskets. She'd been warned by the sanitation police dozens of times, and all they got for their admonitions were a string of curses in Italian. The litter baskets were for papers and cigarette wraps, she was told, and not for household garbage.

They explained to her that she could get a summons for depositing her garbage in the basket. She'd listen attentively, and when the lecture was finished, she'd curse the lecturer's mother, father, children, and anyone else he knew or would ever meet.

She beckoned Jake closer to her with her gnarled and arthritic right hand. He didn't like to get too close because he felt that she smelled. "Whata ya want, Frieda? Do you know where everyone went? The place is empty."

"He's dead! I can tell!" she rasped with her witch's voice, cracking as she spoke. "He was dead on the sidewalk. I told Charlie the Cop, but he just told me to get back. Helen went for the priest, but it wasn't any use. He's dead. I told his wife too, but she wouldn't listen. Helen went to the hospital with her, and Pat's at the house with the kids."

He was just starting to speak when the phone rang. He paused for a second, looking at Frieda, and then decided to answer the phone.

CHAPTER 66

"Oh, Jake." It was Helen's voice. "I'm so glad you're home. Joe Becker's had a heart attack. We're at Lutheran. Jake, I think he's gonna die!"

"What happened, Mid?"

"I don't know! He was with Pat and me. He had a cup of coffee, and we talked for awhile. Then he said he was gonna go home. Margie and he were gonna go to Eighty-Sixth Street and do some shopping. He let himself out, and the next thing I knew, Frieda was knocking on the window. I saw Charlie kneeling over him, opening his shirt and calling on his walkie-talkie for an ambulance. He started giving him that mouth-to-mouth breathing stuff. I ran to get the priest for him. By the time we got back, the ambulance was there, and they had oxygen on him. He opened his eyes in the ambulance, and the priest gave him his last rites. Marge is here, and she wants you to come down."

Joe Becker was dead when Jake got there. Charlie Bennet met him at the desk and broke the news to him. Helen and Marge came out of the emergency room with Father Brady from St. Anselem's. Father Tom was consoling Marge as best he could. When she saw Jake, she broke down completely. He sat down and spoke soft words to her. Nothing earth-shattering, just words about Joe and his feelings for him.

He recalled the kindness Joe showed to Middie during the war years and how close his daughters and grandchildren were to Joe. He spoke softly, almost inaudibly, but Marge heard and felt better. They left in a taxi to make arrangements at Clavin's on Seventh-Ninth and Fourth Avenue. Joe Clavin was a close friend of Marge and Joe; he'd do a good job for them.

After the burial, Jake went into a shell. He couldn't get his mind off Joe. So about a week later, Middie hung the sign in the window to notify the customers that the store was closed: "Jake's drunk again."

After three more days, Jake returned to normal. He rationalized that he had mourned his friend in his own way—not by saying prayers and beating his breast with mea culpas, but by drinking and recalling memories of Joe, the way he was when he was alive. Thus, the more he expounded Joe's virtues, the easier it was for him to get used to Joe being gone.

CHAPTER 67

"Who are those young men across the street?" I asked Helen one morning.

"Them? They're the weight lifters. They just rented the store to Irving the Yiddle."

"Wait a minute, Helen. I know you have a name for almost everyone, but Irving the Yiddle? That's a new one even for you."

"You know Irving [she always prefaced her identification of someone in this matter], he owns the fabric store on Eighty-Second Street. Jake named him that. As a matter of fact, my grandson called it to him one morning right here."

"What did he say when the lad said that?"

"Well, for a minute, I thought he'd get annoyed. He doesn't have much of a sense of humor. Anyway, he knows that I really don't give a damn if the kids annoy him or not. Instead, he howled until he had tears coming out of his eyes. He's all right for a…well, you know. Anyways, he owns that store across the street too, and I knew the weight lifters needed a place. So I talked to Irv, and he agreed to let them use it until he could rent it out."

Her logic was undeniable. She continued, "Ya see, this prevents the other kids from vandalizing the neighborhood. It gives the boys a place to work out. It gives protection to the store owners around here, because the weight lifters will keep out any troublemakers that wander into the neighborhood. So everyone, including Irving, will benefit."

I marveled at this very special lady's continued awareness of the neighborhood problems and the genuine concern she had for its young people.

CHAPTER 68

As with anything that was intrinsically good, there were always those who were against it just for the sake of being contrary or plain mean. The arrangement was working out quite well for all concerned. The weight lifters were using the store for the purpose of bettering themselves, both physically and, more recently, mentally. They had begun reading books—no smut (as Helen called it), but contemporary literature. Their facilities were limited. So when all the equipment was in use, the lads that were waiting their turn would read. The books were given to them by people in the neighborhood through Helen.

The fly in the ointment was Mrs. Japier and her son Bruce. She was a widow, and Bruce was a rookie cop who recalled and still resented the treatment he'd received as a child and teenager growing up with the stigma of a drunkard for a father and a domineering mother who was universally disliked. His name, Bruce, was another bone of contention for him that he never overcame, so because of this newfound status as a policeman, he was now donning the mantle of tough guy. The mother, who was forever calling the police and complaining that illegal and immoral activities were going on inside, was getting nowhere because of the "cop" on the beat. He knew the club was good for the kids and the neighbors. He knew the attitude of Bruce. So Officer Bennet protected the club from unfair criticism at the station house, and because of the esteem the other officers held him in, the unfair complaints of this malcontent family fell upon deaf ears.

Bruce knew how to deal with such inefficiency on the part of the local precinct police in general and one officer in particular. His letter, of course, was anonymous, and it was sent to the department's internal affairs section. The letter alleged a payoff to the radio car officers and to the foot patrol officer. It also included that narcotics were being used and sold openly inside the club itself.

At first, the undercover operation was discreet.

The usual police procedure was followed, and a narcotics officer tried to make "a buy" inside the club. But all he got for his attempt was a swift demonstration of the physical prowess that one could develop when one started lifting weights for an extended period of time.

CHAPTER 69

After a three-month clandestine operation proved conclusively that the club was being used for activities of a nonsinister nature, a report was forwarded to the precinct commander, informing him of the nature of the allegations and the results of the investigation. Even before the captain had heard of the report, Charlie the Cop was starting his own investigation into the origin of the letter. The only ones who outwardly spoke against the club were the young cop and his mother, so they were his prime suspects.

Bruce was trying to use his job to impress everyone in the area. He felt he had to make up things about work and brag to the neighborhood kids about these imagined exploits. He realized that the young men in the club saw him for what he was, and he resented their disinterested attitude toward him.

Charlie was quick to realize that the letter was sent by Bruce, but proof was hard to get. For a cop, the thing that was hated the most, besides rain, was a letter writer. And especially if the writer was another cop.

His plan was simple. The anonymous letters would start again if and when he started to enforce the parking regulations against the young officer's auto.

The first summons brought a red-faced man to the Candy Store, demanding to know Bennett's whereabouts.

"Helen, where the hell is that bastard Bennett?"

She immediately turned on him. "Who do you think you are? I never gave you permission to call me by my first name. You call me Mrs. Ryan, and don't ever come in here that way again, you snotty little bastard."

"You can't talk to me that way. I'm a cop! You can't talk to me that way!"

"Go damn in your cop's hat."

Still red-faced, he left.

"Helen, you're an—"

She held up her hand to silence Charlie. He'd heard everything that went on while making use of Helen's lavatory facility. He knew he could expect to be called on the carpet, but he'd settle the question as to whether or not Japier was the letter writer and how to fix him if he was the guilty one.

CHAPTER 70

"Well, hello, Dan! It's been long time. Sit down, and I'll make some fresh coffee. My, my, you look grand."

"Helen, this isn't really a social call. I'm sorry, but—"

"You can talk later. Now have a roll and butter, and tell me where you've been."

Pat came from the apartment and nearly had a coronary. She was in blue jeans and a sweatshirt, and her hair was pulled back with a red bandanna.

He spied her immediately and stood up. "Pat, how nice to see you. I'm so sorry I have had to break both those appointments. I've been transferred to a new assignment, and I've been real busy. I go around to all the boroughs now, and my hours are uncertain. So in a way, I'm apologizing. I hope you'll understand."

"Dan, there's no explanation necessary. I didn't expect to hear from you so soon anyway." She was getting flustered again and could feel herself getting.

Helen pushed a buttered role and coffee in front of him, and the conversation changed. "Dan, you're not a detective sergeant anymore?"

"Yes. I still am, but I have a temporary assignment. I'm here because of the letters written about Charlie Bennett. It's also about the storefront across the street. Helen, I have to investigate this. Even though Charlie is my friend, I'm going to do a thorough job."

"I know you will, Dan. Let me tell you who the bastard is that wrote the letters. He is a cop and a stupid ass."

She launched into the background of Bruce and gave a good insight to Dan about the formerly anonymous informant. The rest was mere procedure. A check of the handwriting of Japier proved conclusively that he wrote all the letters. Inspection of the club also proved, as did the narcotic investigation, that no immoral or illegal activities were taking place. Interviews with area residents and merchants revealed a fine rapport between the weight lifters and those interviewed. A discreet surveillance of Officer Bennet revealed what Dan already knew, that he was an honest, fair, and capable officer—a credit to the department (as Helen was fond of saying).

As for the young rookie, he was called to the area inspector's office and was questioned about the club, Bennett, and lastly, the letters. He denied knowing anything about anything. Dan requested that he be returned to his normal detective duties because he felt that he'd be prejudiced if it were left to him to select or recommend the punishment to be given to the "young punk"—not his words, but Helen's.

CHAPTER 71

After Bennett and the weight lifters were cleared, things quickly returned to normal on Third Avenue. Dan came to the store more frequently, and Pat smiled and laughed more than she had for quite some time. Helen, of course, had a master plan working, and she knew in her heart (and hoped in her head) that everything would work out just swell.

This was a time of the year that lasted but a few days, when things in general around the store were very quiet. The quietness was not due to a slack period of business or a lack of interest in the people and their problems by Helen and Jake. It was a kind of solemnity that one who was familiar with their routine could sense more than see. Oh, the smile was still there, and the jokes flowed but only one way—from the "regulars" to the Ryans—but nothing came back, no retort. It's usually written off with "Well, I guess they're entitled to a bad day once in a while."

This past February, I had come back from the coast after a mixed golfing and business trip, and as usual I stopped in the store. I was greeted by Helen very warmly. After the routine questions, she became very quiet, almost pensive. Wally came in and nodded to me and gave Helen an extralong embrace. He just looked at Jake and shook his head. Except for the fact that I knew them so well (or at least I thought I did), I probably wouldn't have noticed. None of the other patrons seemed to. Could I be imagining things, or was something wrong?

I had to find out. So I ordered another coffee, and when Helen gave it to me, I asked her if there was a problem that I could help with. Besides looking at me like I was the owner of two heads, she told me I was imagining things, probably I was affected by jet lag. Finishing the coffee, I felt better but couldn't shake the vibrations that had come over me.

CHAPTER 72

The bar was crowded when I entered. There was an unusual amount of noise, and smoke hung in midair. It looked like the view from the Promenade in Brooklyn Heights toward the city when one could actually see the smog just hanging over the skyline. I remembered a similar scene last year, and it was just about this time too. I might have been daydreaming. But something made the Ryans different this time of year. With these thoughts on my mind, I made my way toward the restaurant area and beckoned to Bob Toomey, the maître d'.

Bob was a giant of a man with huge paw-like hands. He was a fixture at the Hamilton House and a great asset to the owners. He would never forget a face and very rarely a name. My table, looking out onto the Verrazano-Narrows Bridge, was, as usual, waiting, and he and I chatted as we walked to it together. I thanked him for keeping the reservation, and then for no explainable reason, I just asked Big Bob if he knew Jake and Helen. Now, my business was asking questions, and I'd made a good living from reading people's reactions to my questions, but the expression that came on Toomey's face left me completely lost and puzzled.

He seated himself and started to tell me about Jake and Helen and why this was a "special" time of year for them.

CHAPTER 73

Betsy was the oldest and the prettiest, according to Bob. She was beautiful. I knew that they had five daughters. I had met four, and I just assumed that the other died when she was a child. Bob told me what had happened.

Betsy was out of high school about four years and was working as a secretary in the Telephone Company. She, as I mentioned, was beautiful and intelligent. One day in the company cafeteria, she was spotted by a gentleman from the company's public relations department. He was quite taken by her features. After identifying himself and obtaining the name of her supervisor, he excused himself and left. She, thinking nothing more of it other than a man wanting to say hello, continued on about her daily routine as two weeks passed. One Tuesday morning, she was told to go to the director of personnel's office on the twenty-fifth floor. Entering, she told the receptionist who she was and was immediately ushered into a large conference room with rich paneled mahogany walls. Seated at the table were fourteen men, including the one from the cafeteria. They all rose and nodded to her as one man showed her to a chair at the extreme end of the table. As she sank lightly into the soft leather, she momentarily thought that it was a pleasant way to be fired.

Finally, the man from the cafeteria reintroduced himself and proceeded to introduce the other men at the table. She realized that they were the board of directors. She'd typed their names many times and had seen their pictures adorning the walls of the building. Of course, she'd never seen them in person before.

"Ms. Ryan, I realize you must be wondering why we're here."

What an understatement, she thought.

"So I'll get right to the point. We of the phone company are looking to project a new image—a young, fresh, and wholesome image. In keeping with the times, we want to place an emphasis on youth. Alexander Graham Bell has been dead for a great number of years now, and we want to get away from the old image of high collars and upsweep hairstyles. We've gone to the modeling agencies and have looked at literally thousands of photos of young ladies. We've selected girls of every ethnic background for their looks. They will be used on posters and in magazines. Why you're here is simple. You are a very beautiful young lady. Personnel records show your absentee record is well below average. Your supervisors think highly of you, as do your coworkers. Your appearance is excKathleent, and you have a high IQ.

"We of the board want to make you our link with youth. You'll go to colleges up and down the entire coast, recruiting young people for careers with the company. Of course, you will get a raise, and a company automobile would be furnished for you. There will be many advantages for you, and you'll see them as you get further involved in the job. If we prove successful with our recruiting, we'll then go into high schools and try to attract the non-college-minded young men and women. Quite frankly, Ms. Ryan, we feel fortunate that you come from within our ranks, so to speak, because it will be easier for you to describe the benefits of working for the phone company."

She sat there stunned, not knowing what to do or say.

The spokesman continued, "You don't have to give us your decision today, but we'd appreciate knowing your thoughts by week's end."

One balding man rose and gently slipped her chair from beneath her as she stood. Each executive individually shook her hand and said it would be a wonderful opportunity for her and that she'd be wise to accept.

That night at dinner, she told her family of the offer and that she thought she'd like to accept it and asked what her parents thought of the idea. Helen wanted to know how much of a raise it meant, where she would live, when she would be traveling, and who would watch out for her. She kept up with the barrage of questions until Jake interrupted, "Do you think you'll be able to handle it?"

"Yes, sir, Daddy, I do."

"Then do it."

Her decision was made, and after a two-week orientation, she left on her first assignment at an all-girls college in Maryland. At first she was nervous, but as soon as she stood before the assembled students, she took complete charge. Her demeanor was perfect, her delivery was superb, and the question-and-answer period at the end was interesting as it was witty. She knew that she had given a good presentation and felt proud.

At the time of her promotion, she had dates anytime she wanted. There were three young men in particular that she'd alternate her free time with. Helen and Jake had met them, as they had met all the young men the girls dated. They didn't insist that they not see specific boys, but the daughters could tell the ones they approved of and the ones they didn't. Betsy was at the stage where she wanted to get married but was enjoying the attention being shown to her by the young hopefuls that continually phoned her.

CHAPTER 74

Her job was progressing nicely, and she found the experiences exciting as well as rewarding. On one road trip to Boston University, she met Jack Lynch, a running back with the New York Giants football team. As big as he was, he was very gentle and soft-spoken. It was a reunion for his class and the start of a marvelous weekend for Betsy.

She was walking from the administration building to Founders Hall. She had her heat down to protect her hairstyle from the wind, and she walked right into Lynch's chest. After the apologies were over, she took the initiative and queried, "Don't I know you from someplace?"

"That should be my line to you."

"No, really, you look very familiar. I know I've seen you someplace before."

He introduced himself, and she immediately realized who he was. She was an avid sport enthusiast but more so for all the hometown teams. She knew betting averages as well as football stats. She remembered goals scored by individual players and many other pieces of sports-related information, which was uncommon for a girl. From then on, he and she spent all their free time together.

At the dean's reception that evening, all eyes focused on them as they entered the hall—he in a dark-blue business suit and she in a Kelly green gown that clung to her as if it had been made expressly for her alone. Her white teeth were gleaming, and her black hair was lying on her shoulders, reflecting the color of her dress and the light from the chandeliers.

Their upbringing was different as could be. Jack was an only child of wealthy parents. They owned a palatial home in Garden

City, Long Island. He was the product of private schools and lack of parental love or interest.

Betsy was one of five from a Brooklyn cold-water flat. She had gone, as did the other girls, to OLPH Grammar School and then to St. Brendan's, the all-girls diocesan high school.

Jack's education had cost thousands upon thousands of dollars. Betsy's had been free except for the weekly collection and a few fund-raising drives that took place from time to time. But together, they talked on subjects touching on philosophy, music, and mythology. Once he met Helen and Jake, he was convinced that his bachelor days were soon to be over (if she'd have him). The girl without the parents would have been enough to make him ask for her hand, but once he met her parents, he wanted to be totally involved. He wanted marriage.

CHAPTER 75

One Thursday morning, she walked into the administration building of the CW Post College on Long Island. As was her custom, she wanted to thank the dean of students personally for all the courtesies he and the staff had extended to her during her stay at the school. She was informed she'd have to wait for a brief time, so she seated herself and began leafing through a sports magazine. Her eyes was carelessly wandering the length and width of the reception room when she suddenly felt dizzy. A wave of nausea swept over her, and she had trouble focusing on fixed objects. The receptionist quickly handed her a glass of water, which Betsy was barely able to raise to her lips.

With the aid of the receptionist, she made it to the nurse's quarters, where she literally fell onto the cot. After about a half hour later, she felt better. The dizziness and nausea had passed, and her composure was regained. It was a Friday, so she knew she'd get plenty of rest over the weekend, as Jack was away at training camp and she had stopped dating anyone else. This was the fourth such spell she'd had like this in the past six months. She discounted them as a result of being overly tired. This one did concern her because it lasted longer than the others had.

She made up her mind that she was going to have a complete physical (someday).

The next six months flew for Betsy. She was in love, and she was happy. The football season was exciting, but the road games and training sessions curtailed her seeing Jack as much as she wanted to. Helen became a real football nut, and every play that Jack was part of, she'd yelp and hoot as if she were at the stadium. Jake had always liked football, but now he'd comment to the TV set on Sundays when the Giants were caught offsides or for any other infractions.

The last day of January brought with it cold and rain. There was something else that came along also. Jack and Betsy had agreed that, after the season, they'd formally announce their engagement, although everyone knew it was a foregone conclusion. Contract negotiations had begun almost as soon as the season ended, and as Jack was named All Pro, he'd be getting a raise in salary. Everything was settled, and Jack had the ring.

The team quarterback, Patty O'Leary, and his wife had arranged a party for Betsy and Jack at their home in Glen Ridge, New Jersey. Helen, Jake, the girls, and their dates were invited. The house was magnificent. There were sandwiches of every description, drinks for any taste or desire. Jake chuckled to himself when he realized that all these men he'd been watching on television for years were just regular guys—nothing "put on" or fancy about them. He liked them and the young ladies that were with them. Patty was a perfect host and a considerate one also. Because of the inclemency of the weather, he started a fire in the huge hearth that was the living-room wall. Within minutes, the house was filled by the warmth of the fire and the congeniality of the company.

Helen, Mrs. O'Leary (Pat's mother), Erin, and Tara were seated in the living room near the fireplace. Betsy had seated herself on the floor next to her mother, and all were engaged in an animated conversation.

Jake walked in from the kitchen with a cup of coffee for Helen and tea for Betsy. He stood in the doorway, looking at the women. He started to feel himself choking up. The light from the fire was actually bouncing off Betsy's dark silken hair, and her eyes shone like the proverbial diamonds. The flames changed her skin from soft white to copper, to orange, then to a sort of hue that you saw surrounding pictures of angels.

A sadness came over him along with a sense of pride. She sensed him looking at her. She turned full face toward him and, smiling that white smile of hers, winked at him He winked back and felt a bit of moistness around his eyes. He reflected, briefly, on how fortunate he was to have them.

About a month after the party, Betsy was still on cloud nine, and she infected the rest of the family with her happiness.

"Where are you off to tonight, Betsy?"

"Well, Kathy Hampton had another baby, and I do want to just go to the hospital to say hello. Remember the time I had my appendix attack? She came to see me, and she was four days overdue with her third."

"How many days does this make now?" Kathleen asked.

"This is her fifth."

Helen nodded her approval of having children and then suggested that Betsy not go. "After all, the weather is lousy, and I'm sure she'll be there again. You know how that guy she's married to gets."

Betsy laughed at her mother's remark and told her, "I'm going to tell Frank what you said, Mother."

"Don't you dare. I'm only fooling. He is a good Catholic man."

Jake muttered something about a "sex fiend," and they all laughed.

CHAPTER 76

She left the house after kissing her mother and father. "I'll only be gone about an hour. I just want to see Kathy and the baby and show her my ring. I think she's the only one who hasn't seen it. Oh, I'm so happy. Tomorrow, I am going to rent the Electric Billboard at Times Square and tell the whole world!"

Walking from the elevator to her friend's room, she began to have difficulty keeping things in focus. She felt nauseous. She'd had the feelings before, but never as severe as now. She woke up in a bed next with sides on it at the hospital. Jake and Helen were seated next to her, and Jack was standing at the foot of the bed.

"Mother! What happened? Where am I?" She turned to Jack. "Jack, what's wrong?" But he turned and looked away. "Daddy, please, tell me what's the matter! Daddy, *please*!"

The doctors had told Jake everything about her condition. They felt it would be easier if one of her family told her what was wrong. As the doctor in charge had said, "The human approach is what's needed now, not the clinical approach."

"Honey, I...I...Look, do you remember when you were little and I always told you and the others not to lie to your mother and me?"

She nodded but with a puzzled look on her face. He started to continue but couldn't help but think how beautiful she was even though her face was devoid of any makeup.

"Well, I told you then that I'd never lie to you either. Do you remember that? Well, I'm not going to lie to you now." He gripped her milk-white hand in a firm but soft hold. "Honey, you have leukemia."

The word hit her with the force of a giant cudgel. She looked at Jack then to Helen. Helen was weeping softly, and Betsy touched her hand.

"Mom, please don't. It won't do any good. Please don't! Please, Mom."

Composing herself, Middie looked at her daughter and managed to smile.

CHAPTER 77

The prognosis was that she had probably five to six months, at best, before the disease would take over and eventually claim her. Jack wanted to get married immediately and try to soothe the inevitable for his Betsy. She, being and thinking pragmatically, vetoed the idea. She understood his feelings but felt that the burden she'd become would outweigh their moments of joy together. She went to the Cancer Research Center in the city and volunteered to submit to any tests or research projects that were in the offing and needed a human for experimentation.

The doctors had termed her case as "terminal without hope of remission." She felt that her remaining time could be spent constructively, helping to find the reasons why people contracted the disease, what could be done to prevent it, and what could be done to find a cure. Although she knew that hers was a hopeless case, maybe she could be of some small help to someone else.

The whole family tried to continue as if everything was normal. The Phone Company wanted her to stay on as an administrative consultant. She'd only be required to go to training seminars once a week. The thought was nice, but she declined. With the exception of the time she spent with Jack, she became totally immersed in the work and experiments at the research center. The scientists were working with a segment of the blood called platelets. They weren't sure what effect, if any, the platelets had on victims of the disease. They had, through laboratory research, realized that this element of the blood was necessary in forming clots. This was the way the chief doctor in charge of research, a crew-cut doctor Fred Cross by name, explained it: "We know it produces clots in the blood of animals, but what will happen in humans is another side of the coin."

"What you are offering to me and my team is a scientist's dream. Ms. Ryan, I'd be a liar if I said there was hope for regression in your case. I've studied this for ten years, and unfortunately, I will need ten more. But if we can, through you, be able to get at least a step closer to a cure, then with the help of God, we'll save other people from… Well, what I mean is…I'm sorry I sound so clinical, but with your help maybe—and it's just that, a maybe—we can in the future save others."

Betsy dived right into the project, as did the rest of the family, except for Pat. Because of her age, the doctors couldn't take her blood for analysis. Not only the defensive line but the offensive line of the Giants leapt into the experiment. Not to belabor the scene with the technical aspects of the experiment, it should suffice to say that Betsy's contribution helped immensely. But time ran out for the dark-haired beauty, and Betsy eventually died.

Helen and the rest of them still gave platelets once a week. Through the research and the use of the clotting factor, untold thousands were now leading normal functional lives with the hope of regression and the possibility of a cure.

Although she died fifteen years ago, her death contributed to the furtherance of a possible cure for the disease. We'd probably never now how much, but it was enough for her family to know that it wasn't in vain. And it was enough for me to know that I'd been blessed with the opportunity to know such exceptional people.

CHAPTER 78

To all our friends, next Saturday and Sunday, Monday, and Tuesday, we will be closed for business. Pat is getting married, and you know how Jake will probably get. So we'll see you on Wednesday. Helen and Jake.

There hadn't been this much excitement in the Ryan family since Jake came home from the war. Dan wanted Pat to be as happy as he could possibly make her. He was, by nature, a quiet man. Never before had he known such a family. Everything they did was virtually attacked with a type of energy that if harnessed, would light Lower Manhattan. The sisters, aunts, cousins, neighbors, and everyone were infected with a type of happiness and joy that Dan had never been exposed to.

Jake, of course, was his usual unflappable self! He'd go along with anything. Middie would get annoyed at him, but he'd smile and then send a wink. They had a line of communication that was always open. Although Helen interspersed her love with curse words, it was pure love, nonetheless.

The guest list was unreal. It ran from Uncle Lulu to Bishop Dooley of Brooklyn. Pat was telling Dan who each one was and, like her father, gave a little background on each guest.

"Now, Uncle Lulu. He's really not my uncle, but he's my mother's cousin. He drinks a lot, but he's really a good man at heart. He has a pension from World War I and Social Security, and sometimes he gets arrested, but Aunt Maisie promised to keep him clean and sober for the day.

"Now, Aunt Maisie is my aunt. She's my mother's sister, but Lulu lives in a room in her house, and he listens to her. Next we have Rocco DiBello. He is an old friend of my father's. He owned a sandwich shop near the pier that Daddy worked at years ago. He's a real nice man. I could never understand why my father is always so nice to him. I mean, you know how he talks about people's nationalities, yet I can never remember him making an ethnic remark to Mr. Rocco. And for Daddy, that's remarkable."

"Honey, who's Mrs. Harris?"

"Oh, you'll love her. That's Queenie. That's my father's name for her."

"Why Queenie?"

"She was a showgirl in New York and Hollywood. She was in two movies, you know, in the chorus of the Fred Astaire and Ginger Rogers spectaculars. They've been on the *Late Show* dozens of times."

"Where'd the 'Queenie' come in?"

"Well, according to my father, she was really a burlesque queen who became a madam until recently. The only reason she retired was because she broke her hip. So he dubbed her Queenie, as in burlesque queen."

Dan was enjoying the list and the story behind each and every guest. He sat there looking at this girl, and his heart was pounding. Outwardly, he was calm, but inside, his very soul was bursting with the joy that could come to one who had found what he'd been looking for all his life.

"Pat," he finally asked, "one thing has been puzzling me. How did the bishop of Brooklyn get involved? I know that your mother and father are remarkable people and know almost everyone and their brother—but I mean, the bishop?"

"My father and your grandfather were friends of the bishop's father. My parents were invited to his elevation ceremony. He's been here at the store many times. In fact, when we found out George was really dead, he said a special Mass. If it's all right with you, he wants to say our Mass."

"I think it would be an honor, and it would please me very much. I have some news for you. Remember when we first met and started talking? I told you I had taken another promotion exam. Well—"

"Oh, Dan, you passed? Oh, wonderful! Oh, it's great! You're going to be a lieutenant."

She leaped into his arms and smothered him with warm, happy kisses. Helen came from the kitchen at the sound of the happy commotion. As she viewed the scene, tears started to well up in her eyes. She knew that all the surreptitious prodding and praying she had done all these months was bearing the fruit she'd hoped for. Only six more days and her daughter and her children would be safe and happy once again. He had a nice face. He must take after his grandfather.

Dan went to work as usual and immersed himself in the many investigations his unit was conducting. At lunchtime, he stopped to call Pat. Helen answered and told him that Pat was called to the school principal's office at St. Anselm's. The principal, Sister Cecelia James, had phoned and asked Pat to come to her office. She wanted to talk about the ten-year-old sixth grader's attitude and manner.

CHAPTER 79

Helen wasn't an alarmist, but he did detect more than matriarchal concern in her voice, so he asked directly if she knew what the meeting pertained to.

"I don't know, Dan, but he's been acting goddamn queer for the past three weeks. I thought I was imagining things, but I guess I was right."

"Helen, have I missed something? Do you think it's because of the wedding?"

"I don't know. But if you ask me, a swift kick in the ass wouldn't do him any harm."

"I hope you have Pat phone me when she comes back. Now that I think of it, he has been awfully quiet lately."

After asking for Jake and indulging in a little small talk, he said goodbye and hung up. The rest of the day was taken up with his supervisory duties, and he had little time to think about his personal life. About five that evening, he was getting ready to call it a day when he decided to call Pat.

"Hello, dear, how'd your day go?"

"Oh, Dan, Mother told me you called. I don't know what to do! It's George. He told Sister that he wants to leave home. He says I hate him and that I hate his father too. Dan, I'm so upset. I don't know what to do."

"Listen, Pat, and calm down." His voice took on an unfamiliar firmness, and she immediately stopped talking. "I'm coming over, and we'll talk all this over. Where's George now?"

"He's out in the store with my father. Dan, he won't speak to me at all. My mother says I should punish him but..."

"Don't to that, honey. I'll be over in a half, however. Wash his face and comb his hair. I'm going to take him out with me if it's all right with you."

"Of course, it's all right, dear."

CHAPTER 80

As he drove from his office, he reflected on George and what he thought the lad's problem might be. Calmly, and with some sadness, he started to think about what it must be like for a nine-year-old who never knew his father to be torn from the world of hero worship and forced into the real world of seeing an "ordinary" man making his mother smile and laugh. He knew that was the lad's problem. How could he have been so blind? How could he have been so selfish? The kid had a right to be mad. He was so concerned with his and Pat's happiness that he'd forgotten about her children's feelings.

He stopped a few blocks from the store and tried to formulate his thoughts. He wanted to be able to "sell" himself to the lad. The more he thought about the selling idea, the less he liked it. He wanted her children to accept him for now. He felt that their love would come later, in time.

George didn't offer any resistance to going with Dan. He didn't ask where they were going and spoke only when Dan directly asked him questions. All the children were polite and well-mannered. This was due largely to the discipline enforced by Pat. Helen was strong, but like Jake, she exercised discipline as a grandparent's prerogative and bordered on spoiling the children. He stopped the car in Sheepshead Bay at the ferry to Breezy Point.

"Would you mind riding the ferry with me, George? I always think better in fresh air."

"If you want, Mr. McCarthy."

He purchased two tokens, and they walked the length of the dock to the tiny ferryboat. The April evening was warm and windless. The sun was bouncing off the stagnant dockside water. The reflection hid the oil slicks and raw waste from view. Dan caught George looking into the silvery water and noticed a pleased look on the boy's face.

"Have you ever been on a ferryboat, George?"

"No, sir, I haven't."

"When I was a few years older than you, I worked on a ferry every summer for five years."

"Really?" The boy seemed interested.

"Yes, as a matter of fact. We had a bungalow in Breezy Point, and I got myself a job. I kept it until I joined the Marines."

The boy's head spun so quickly Dan thought he'd hurt himself.

"Of course," he continued, "I wasn't in any war like your father, but you have to understand that Korea was over and Vietnam hadn't started."

The boy started to speak but then stopped. Dan didn't speak either. Suddenly, the lad looked at Dan and asked in a quizzical tone, "Did you ever kill anyone?"

The frankness of the question took him by surprise. He didn't want to lie to the youth, nor did he relish the thought of having to divulge his police exploits to win acceptance from his stepson-to-be.

"George, I don't want to take your father's place in your eyes. I'd just appreciate it if you'd give me a chance to show you how much I love your mother and how much I'm willing to take care of you and the other children. Your father was a brave and patriotic man. He gave his life so that this country would remain free. I don't want nor do I expect your mother or anyone else to forget him and what he did for all of us. It's hard now for you to understand just how your mother can marry an ordinary man when your dad was such a hero. I realize this, and so does your mother. I don't even expect you to call me dad. I just want the chance to give your family the love and protection that your father would want them to have."

He had hoped for some sigh of understanding from the youth, but none was forthcoming. The return ride was made in silence. When the boat docked in Sheepshead Bay, the man and the boy walked the length of the pier in silence. As they headed toward the car, Dan was searching for words. Unexpectedly, he felt George touch his fingers and opened his hand wide. The little blond boy curled his fingers inside the safety of Dan's strong left hand. He said a slight prayer of thanksgiving, for he knew the boy understood.

CHAPTER 81

"Well, the time's almost here."

"Yep, only three more days, and I'll be losing my little girl and her children. I'm not sad, though, because she's getting a wonderful guy."

Helen was smiling, but I knew she'd miss them all. She, for all her outward toughness, was one of the kindest, gentlest, and most considerate people I'd ever met. The people in the neighborhood had a lot to be thankful for when she and Jake took over the Candy Store. Everything they did, from selling a pack of cigarettes to raising money for the school for special-needs children, was done with such zeal and ambition that one couldn't help getting involved either overtly or inadvertently. There was, for example, the time that the city had cut back the aid to the School for Exceptional Children.

Helen had heard of the school and always donated soda, candy, or ice cream whenever they had a party or "just for the hell of it." She'd never been to the storefront school but was friendly with the director, Tony Cavalier. One day, Tony came to the store and started telling her about the fiscal woes they were having. The city had reneged on a deal that had been agreed to but not in writing: for every three dollars that the school would raise, the city would supply two dollars. The only stipulation was that the school had to post a $10,000 security bond against any lawsuits that the city would be held accountable for. The school raised the sum, but the powers that be at city hall held that because of the fact that the school was predominately white, it had to back out of the deal. The fact that the school serviced over two hundred families was of no consequence. There just wasn't the proper minority makeup for the city to expend any money. Without the money, the school would surely close, and the special-needs children and their families would be left to fend for themselves.

"Those bum bastards! They have some goddamn nerve. What are these kids supposed to do without that place? I don't know much about minorities, but I think that those kids are a kind of minority themselves. The colored people around here should be thankful that their kids don't need that kind of school. What the frig is wrong with those people in city hall? We should be able to do something about this."

Jake walked into the store just as Helen had finished her statement, and he mumbled, "Here we go again."

The first step in her plan was to organize the other candy-store owners to withhold their newspaper payments to *The News*, *The Times*, and *The Post*. In the area surrounding the school, there were forty-three candy stores.

Forty-one of them cooperated. Her reasoning was sound, and two weeks later, an editorial appeared in *The News*, condemning the city. *The Times* was less vociferous but nonetheless also came out for the school and against the reasons the city expressed for not helping the school. *The Post* took the stand for the school but suggested an investigation be conducted into possible corruption in city hall (no one could figure out where the connection was, but that was *The Post*).

The next step was to deluge city hall and the neighborhood with literature explaining the need and further explaining why there were so few minority children in the school. The answer was simple. The neighborhood was mainly white middle class. To bus a special child to the school would be medically unsound and, furthermore, would defeat part of the curriculum of the school. The students were taken daily on walking tours of the neighborhood. Each was taught how and when to cross the streets near their homes.

Each was taught how to get to their homes in the area and where to get help if they needed it. If students from other neighborhoods were involved, it would clearly lead to confusion for them. They'd be familiar with an area they did not have a need to know. Further, if the minority students were excluded from the vital tours, it would emotionally hurt them to be left out of an activity that the rest of their peers were engaging in.

CHAPTER 82

The circulars were prepared by the kids in the printshop at Fort Hamilton High. There were Danny, Billy, Rocco, Starchy, Gary, Eddie, Dopey Duffy, Finnegan, Glen; they all had a hand in the printing and distribution of the information to the neighborhood. The ball was rolling.

The local papers kept the pressure going. Assemblymen, councilmen, and even a congressman jumped in, voicing their support. The only problem was the city's fear of a lawsuit based on a racial issue.

One sunny afternoon, help came. The *Amsterdam Times* sent a representative to the school. The *Amsterdam Times* had the largest circulation of any black-owned and operated paper in the United States. For years, it had been in the forefront, promoting equal rights for blacks. The black community read and headed most of the views that the paper expounded.

They sent Mr. Clyde Crabbe to the store with Tony Cavalier, and Helen and Jake started explaining their feelings about the school. Neither one of them had much dealings with Negro people, and like some whites, they felt uncomfortable talking to them at first. This was one time Helen didn't want anything to go wrong. She realized immediately how important the support of this paper would mean to their cause.

They closed the store and invited Clyde and Tony into their apartment for coffee. Mr. Crabbe already had lunch at the school with Tony and the children, so he declined Helen's offer of a sandwich. Jake was trying to read him. He thought that this black-faced man must be a fantastic poker player. He couldn't make heads or tails of the pleasant expression on his face. Helen was getting out the good china cups when Jake abruptly spoke.

"Hey, Clyde, would you like a beer?"

She thought her heart had stopped. She looked at Tony, who was busy looking at the scene. She thought of hitting Jake, but...

"That sounds great, Jake. I'd love one."

"I thought you would. Do you want a glass, or is the can good enough?"

"For Christ's sake, Jake, get him a glass!"

"No, I always drink it from a can at home. Listen, would you mind if I take off my jacket and loosen my tie?"

It was all uphill after that. The paper condemned the City Hall, wished the school luck, and sent a $500 donation to aid them. They didn't let it drop there either. Articles were printed daily about the school and the people in it. They, with the others, finally got the city to agree to their bargain and in writing. The school was saved.

Helen spoke (as usual), for Jake declined to accept praise for being the catalyst in the movement. Tony knew she and Jake were sincere in their feelings. So one day, simply and without ceremony, he handed her a gaily wrapped box. She opened it and pushed back the tissue paper. Lying in the box was a wall plaque stating simply:

> To Helen and Jake Ryan, in thankful appre-
> ciation from the exceptional children to excep-
> tional people.

She turned away and wiped her eyes. Jake walked over to his icebox for a beer.

CHAPTER 83

T he sun was shining brilliantly. The sky was picture-perfect blue. The day was made for happiness. Her sisters were fussing and primping. The children, all dressed, were sitting on the couch in the living room. Helen had threatened to "break their friggin legs" if they got dirty before the mass was over.

In the midst of all the confusion, the phone rang, and young George was told to answer it.

"Hello, George, this is Dan. May I speak to your mother, please?"

"Sure. How you doing? Boy, you wouldn't believe what's going on around here. Girls all over the place! Will I be glad when you and Mom get back. At least with you and Grandpa, we'll have the upper hand."

"You can bet on that, George."

The lad's tone of voice bolstered Dan's spirits. They were going to hit it off just fine.

"Hello, dear, happy wedding day!"

"Hi, Dan, same to you. Are you all set? I mean, are all the fellas there? You're not calling to tell me you made an arrest and can't make it today?"

"Well, honey, that's just why I called. You see, we have this investigation going, and we're going to make an arrest at about one o'clock. I know you'll understand. We'll do this, oh, maybe next week. Tell Bishop Dooley to arrange his schedule, and we can put a note on the front door of the church. People will understand."

"You, you! If I tell my mother, do you know what she'd say?"

"Please, I'm only fooling. The last thing I need is for your mother to 'puck me in my eye'!"

They both started laughing at the conversation and Dan's usage of Helen's favorite expression.

He became serious, and Pat listened attentively. "Pat, I love you, and I'm going to do my best to measure up to what you deserve. I've never been as happy as I am today. I know I sound redundant, but I can't help just telling you I love you. You've made me a very happy man."

"Oh, Dan. I know how you feel because I feel the same. I'm as happy as any bride can be. I may even be happier. I'll see you at the church, sweetheart."

"Goodbye, dear. See you in church."

CHAPTER 84

Dan arrived at St. Anselm's thirty minutes early. Guests were already starting to file into the church. The altar was bedecked with bunches of spring daisies surrounded by white and yellow roses. The inside of the church was filled with the aroma of spring and joy.

From a far corner, he stood with his best man, Charlie Bennett, and he watched the people being escorted down the aisle to their seats. He saw old family friends and new friends. These were people he'd met through Pat, Helen, and Jake—people he liked immediately.

A tall slender man with white hair approached Dan and Charlie. Dan extended his hand, giving and receiving a warm response.

"Mr. Phelan, how are you?"

"Hello, Dan, Charlie. Dan, I just want to… Dan, I want you to know that Martha and I are extremely pleased and proud to…er, well… Dammit, Dan, the last time we were this happy… Oh nuts, I knew I'd foul things up."

"Mr. Phelan, I know what you're trying to tell me, and I appreciate it more than you know. I'm glad you and Mrs. Phelan have accepted me."

"Well, Dan, we feel like you are our son. I think the cliché would be something like this: George would be happy for you both."

"I know the Mass and the day will be hard for you and your wife, but by you being here and Mrs. Phelan being at Pat's house, somehow I know George does approve."

He meant it and felt it. The sincerity of his remarks was apparent and appreciated. The two men smiled and again exchanged arm handshakes.

CHAPTER 85

The organist started the traditional prewedding march music as Helen started down the aisle, escorted by two ushers. She was wearing a blue gown, a wristlet of orchids. Her blue eyes sparkled as she winked at Dan. The wedding party started down the main aisle. The young men and women coming single file made a marvelous picture. There was Jerry Feeney, followed by Dan's brother, Dennis, who was followed by their sister, Jennifer; Pat's sister Kathleen; and then Pat's children. The youngest, Timmy, was smiling and waving to everyone. Her matron of honor was her sister Erin.

Then as the bishop, Jake Dooley's son, stood watching, Jake and Pat started down behind the others, and the organist played the wedding march.

She was radiant. She looked at Dan the whole walk. Jake was smiling but slightly nervous. Helen was proud and pleased. This was a day for happiness. "God has been good to Jake and me. I guess we've been lucky," she said to Uncle Wally.

Jake lifted the pink veil and kissed Pat lightly on her freckled cheek. She smiled and kissed him back. He shook Dan's hand and winked. She slipped her arm inside Dan's, and they walked toward the altar. The bishop greeted them, smiling, and started the nuptial Mass. Helen was crying.

Jake was sniffling, and all the other guests were experiencing the same emotions.

When the ceremony was over, the bishop said, "The mass is ended. Go together to love and serve the Lord."

The assemblage answered, "Thanks be to God."

AND SO THEY WERE MARRIED!

ABOUT THE AUTHOR

M r. Hayes is a graduate of Saint Francis College in Brooklyn, New York. Mr. Hayes is a retired sworn police officer who retired after fifty-three years of service in various New York City and state agencies. His wife Janet, and he raised four daughters and have twelve grandchildren. Mr. Hayes was raised in Brooklyn, New York, and still lives in New York City.

This is his second novel, which follows his well-received *Blessed Are the Peacemakers*.

CPSIA information can be obtained
at www.ICGtesting.com
Printed in the USA
BVHW032145021219
565466BV00001B/63/P